ISLINGTON

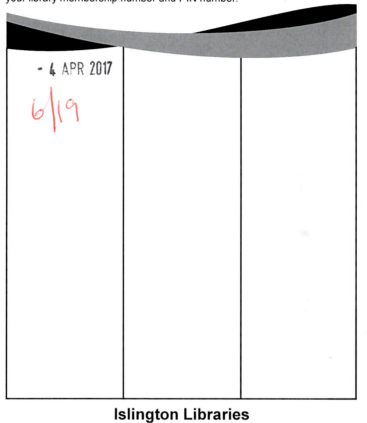

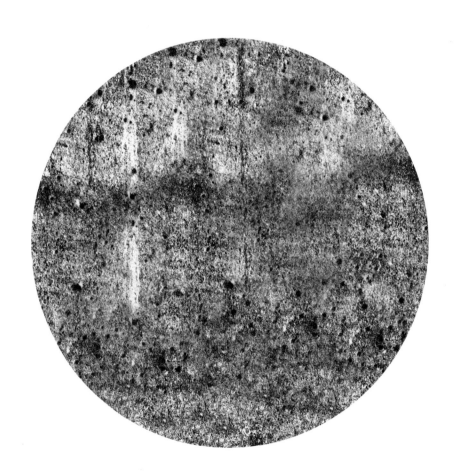

Mortal Cities
Forgotten Monuments

Arna Mačkić

◻◻ PARK BOOKS

Ismet Mačkić, Jasenovac, 1979.

Mortal Cities & Forgotten Monuments started out with me diving into my personal history, but at the same time I touched upon a major complex global issue. I investigated the role architecture played during turning points in the turbulent history of the Balkans, during and after the Second World War as well as during the last Civil War in Bosnia-Herzegovina in 1992-1995. In particular, I focused on the monuments erected by Tito commemorating the battle against fascism, on the lessons we can learn from the way these monuments were designed, and on how their meaning has shifted over the years. With the knowledge I gained from studying these monuments, I came up with a design proposal for the city of Mostar in Bosnia-Herzegovina, which was severely damaged during the war, and is heavily divided today.

How can cities rebuild themselves and how can architecture create peaceful coexistence between different groups of people? How can countries, governments, companies, and cities construct collective identities and inclusive futures through architecture? These questions apply to the many cities that have been confronted by war such as Berlin, Rotterdam, and more recently, Aleppo in Syria. However, due to current shifting demographics, the need to rebuild identities and search for new ways to build inclusive societies also applies to Western European countries and cities.

I wrote the various chapters from my personal view. My family and I fled from the war in Bosnia-Herzegovina in 1993 and we started all over again in the Netherlands. In 1999, when I was eleven, we made our first journey back to the country, which deeply impressed me. That year and the many years after, we visited cities like Mostar and Sarajevo, where I would study the destroyed cities and its demolished buildings. To me, it is a special and unique experience to witness a city like Mostar in such a condition. The cultural heritage that has been demolished or in some places transformed was supposed to tell me something about my identity—which by then was not at all exclusively Yugoslavian or Bosnian.

As for my identity, it was anything but destroyed. Rather, I had gradually become Dutch, but also a little Surinamese, Turkish, Antillean, and all the other cultures and identities with which I was confronted in the massive apartment building we were assigned to after obtaining our residence permit. One reason why I question the issue of identity may well be that I have been an outsider myself. Identities only exist in relation to and in confrontation with the other. Identities are ever changing and never complete and therefore the word identification is more appropriate to describe the unfinished process of relating to others. When rebuilding collective identities through the means of architecture, it is essential to start on the premise that the concept of identity is a process and never complete. Only by recognizing the manifold and multiple realities of collective identities and identifications, can a city be formed that facilitates inclusivity. The first print of *Mortal Cities & Forgotten*

Monuments was published in an edition of only thirty copies to explore the general interest in this topic. Within a year I was invited to hold lectures in various cities: Mostar, Beirut, Stockholm and Amsterdam, proving the global urgency of the issues discussed in this book. Cities that have been subject to demolition and where significant buildings, books, and art have been destroyed are forced to rebuild themselves. They are in a unique position to tell their stories anew and involve their citizens in this process. Using an 'open' design language, as will unfold over the course of this book, is not a simple task, but it is an opportunity to expand architecture for the goal of creating collective, shared, and inclusive identities. Unfortunately, in practice, architecture and heritage are often used to disseminate one particular identity imposed by a ruling power upon the citizens of the demolished city. However, rebuilding collective and inclusive identities through architecture is not a problem that is exclusive to cities affected by war. Western European cities struggle equally with the issue of how they need to deal with citizens and immigrants from different backgrounds, but also how to deal with their sometimes 'charged' national heritage in order to appeal to any citizen. In other words: building inclusivity is a universal problem. The journeys, meetings, and conversations generated by the first edition of *Mortal Cities & Forgotten Monuments* have led to new collaborations and projects that address these questions. Therefore this official edition of Mortal Cities & Forgotten Monuments and the case-study of Mostar needed to be placed in a wider social, historical and governmental context, with the help of the writer and journalist Chris Keulemans, as well as Thomas A. P. van Leeuwen who is a writer and an art and architecture historian, and the design researcher Rosa te Velde, who all relate to my research in their own unique ways. Thanks to the co-authors of this book, I feel we have succeeded in bringing the issues explored into a wider context. This book is also greatly indebted to the legacy

of the architect and urban planner Bogdan Bogdanović (1922-2010). I am very grateful for all their contributions and I feel that *Mortal Cities & Forgotten Monuments* serves as a solid start in exploring how architecture can contribute to building an inclusive society, wherever in the world.

Nura Mačkić and Dubravka Romano, Jasenovac, 1977.

Introduction
by Chris Keulemans

In 1994, Bill Clinton delivered his first State of the Union speech, Krzysztof Kieslowski released *Trois Couleurs: Rouge*, Kurt Cobain committed suicide, Boris Yeltsin ordered troops into Chechnya, genocide swept across Rwanda, and Mostar woke up from two years of siege.

The aftermath was horrific. Entire streets were destroyed beyond recognition. When I passed through in October, I had coffee with a friend in a makeshift bar smelling of damp clothes, sweat, and cheap cigarettes. The place was crammed with weapons and aid packages. Looking through the wide windows, while trying to keep up the conversation with my friend, I felt my language falter. His name was Boro. He was a Bosnian journalist from Sarajevo. He had a dry, light voice that updated me on the war in clipped one-liners. The skin was pulled tight across his bony face. He had not lost his sense of humor. Jokes were everywhere, in those days, but they carried no comfort. I had come to hate the silence that followed. Outside, heavy trucks were plowing through the mud. Of the buildings whose carcasses were left standing, the façades were pock-marked and blinded. Soot blackened the windowsills. It was the large, senseless gaps in between that got me. I found it hard to recover the logic that builds sentences.

On my return to Amsterdam, I wrote a sad book: *From Summer to Reality*. It was about migration, people adrift, and all the misunderstandings that swirl around them. It was also about the Bosnian War, to which there seemed to be no end. Every day, more news of the unimaginable suffering came staggering in. To me, one of the saddest images was that of Bogdan Bogdanović, collapsing into a deep fever when the news reached him that Mostar's Old Bridge had been shelled to pieces. On the day that even the old architect, who had always believed in the eternal life of cities, lost hope, all seemed gone. Bogdanović despaired because the time had come that we were no longer able to read the ancient, the original idea upon which cities had always been built. "This city, born under the sign of the bridge, has been robbed of its first and last word, and its death, I fear, is irrevocable."

In 1999, Arna Mačkić, a child of the city, returned to Mostar when most of the iconic places of her family's history were still in ruins: "The monument designed by Bogdanović commemorating the Partisans who died in World War II, Café Rondo, Hotel Neretva, the Bristol Hotel, the Ruža Hotel, the Razvitak, and Hit department stores, the Gymnasium [secondary school], and the Palace of Culture." This list of names alone invokes a Sebaldesque haunted nostalgia.

"Every single one of these were meaningful public places that made Mostar a vivid, tolerant city where it did not matter what your religion or ethnicity was. One was simply a Mostarac or Mostarka."

Simply? No more. Even such small, innocent words have lost their clarity today. "For me, it has become a dishonest city. The physical annihilation of Mostar has led to its illegibility. [...] If we cannot read the city, we can never reach a higher level: the art of writing a city."

Dictators have written cities. So have real estate magnates and city planners driven by ideology. I visited cities that were brought to ruin in wartime, and saw what writers who don't read will build. Minsk is a spotless, eerie salute to Stalinism. Solidère, in the heart of the Green Zone, the former frontline during Beirut's endless civil war, is a faux-Parisian consumer area without a soul. Recently, glittering shopping malls have been creeping up on Sarajevo's parliament building.

Writing a city is the art of citizens, of human minds sensitive not just to the need of people to sleep, work and eat, but also to spend time with no apparent use, with friends, with strangers who don't need to be distrusted; time that comes and goes. It is an art to create space that can live without a goal or direction. Space that understands itself.

In 1948, the young Swiss writer and architect Max Frisch visited Warsaw, another city in ruins. "Taking a rest in the old town: as if you are the only human being left on earth. In the alleyways, the green of grass, berries growing from empty windows, and when I scramble across the heaps of stone to have a look around, doves flutter up into the air. Silence: as in the grave. As if you're deaf. All around you the quiet that reveals as little as the quiet before an excavation. History as the consciousness of the living."

When he met the young architects planning to rebuild their capital city, he could hardly conceal his optimism. "Much imagination, often on a human scale, sensibility to the cubic rhythm." He crouched over their drawings and saw them dance together to live music in basement bars. "The dancing at night, the building of bridges, the one cannot be thought separately from the other." It is all made possible, he concludes early on, by the new law proclaimed immediately after the war ended, which declared the whole territory of Warsaw to be state property. No more private ownership, no legal obstacles "to build a city for our century."

The result may not have lived up to his expectations. The dangers of state planning—"uniformity, lack of personal style"—took their toll, as he feared. Still, to this day, Warsaw shows how those young post-war architects remained conscious of history and created spaces wide enough for memories to mingle with the present.

Today, it seems, cities have become unwritable. Frisch's optimism is a thing of the past. Authorities have lost their authority, citizens their voice. Writing cities, to rebuild them after war, is now reduced to the scribbling of cheap capitalism, guilty conscience, divided people. No longer is there a unifying story, not even the attempt to find one.

Bogdanović saw it coming. In his beautiful book of essays, *Architektur der Erinnerung* (1994), he wrote: "If Sarajevo is a specific monument to the universality of culture, then I fear that the humiliation she is undergoing today, maybe even its disappearance, will become a new, contrary, dark paradigm. Europe and the whole world should consider seriously what the consequences will be of the destruction of a city like this. Will it not encourage new explosions, new urban destruction from within and without, will it not lead to ethnic, religious, sectarian divisions of city territories, to cultural and especially subcultural divisions?"

One walks outside the monumental centers of European cities like Amsterdam, Brussels, Paris, Berlin, Vienna, and Barcelona, in the neighborhoods that don't appear on tourist maps, and one thinks of the old professor and his sad knowledge of the dividing lines that run through these urban landscapes...

At the end of *From the Summer to Reality*, I proposed an idea. What people share, regardless of culture and background, is the experience of loss. Not an ideology we could share, but the loss of ideology. Not the hope for a future that we can work towards together, but the loss of hope. Not the belief, but the disbelief. Not the conversation, but the loss of the ability to understand each other.

Loss is a strictly personal experience. It cannot be shared. At the same time it is an experience that everyone will know, sooner or later, and recognize. Could we build on that? Could this somehow be the unifying story that pulls our cities back together, and our lives?

Twenty years later, this concept has proven to be hopelessly naive. To work as a collective force, it requires empathy for the loss of others, and that is too much to ask. Look at Bosnia today. Everyone regards his own loss as untouchable. Nobody else is granted access. The memory of lost people and places has become private property. It has solidified. Most people can't seem to get beyond, to overcome.

For a long time, Bosnians repeated their mantra. Once the bridge has been rebuilt, once Karadžić and Mladić are in prison, once I have found the remains of my husband, son, or brother—only then will I be able to make a new start. In the meantime, most of these conditions have been met, although many of the victims are still missing. But the energy to rebuild a true future has evaporated along the way.

Everything has become stained with guilt. New monuments have been erected as tokens of exclusion. Standing at the entrance to the former camp at Trnopolje, where Bosnian women were raped and killed, there is a black eagle with an Orthodox cross—commemorating the Serb soldiers who died in the war. Towering above the Muslim quarter of Mostar is a 100-foot high Catholic cross, illuminated at night. Fortifications of bad conscience, not to be touched, removed, restored—out of fear of new destruction and revenge.

In this climate of mistrust, the Old Bridge was rebuilt on tip-toes, not by new rulers but by foreign peace-makers, meticulously replicating the methods of the Ottoman architect Hajrudin, aware of all the surrounding sensitivities— and however beautiful the result, it no longer feels like a connection, but a separation.

A separation between the two sides of the Neretva river, with the unre- pentant Croatian and Muslim communities opposite each other in a grim travesty of what Bogdan Bogdanović promised when he set out to build the Partisan Necropolis: "How one day, and forever, two cities will face each other, looking into each other's eyes—the city of dead antifascist heroes and the living city for which those heroes gave their lives." After the war, he real- ized this dream would not come true: "All that is left of that original promise is that the former city of the dead and the former city of the living still look at each other—only now they gape with empty, black and scalding eyes."

Today, his tombstone stands in the vandalized necropolis. And the two sides of the city have turned their heads, facing away from each other.

Last year, I came through Mostar again, during a long bus ride across the country. Along the way, the beauty of nature was still overwhelming. But signs that the country has not recovered from the war, twenty years later, were everywhere. Men drinking coffee at forlorn snack bars in the after- noon: there is no work. Houses, new or under reconstruction, abandoned halfway through the building process, floors without a roof, entrances with- out doors: there is no money.

What struck me most was an after-effect that nobody considered when the war was still raging. Foreign powers forged the Dayton Agreement. Bogdanović mourned the irrevocable death of his beloved cities. Political parties and the media kept reproducing the ethnic fault lines long after the war. But of all the evils we could have expected, this was not one of them: the banality. The cheapness, the makeshift repairs, the superficial façades barely covering up poverty and disillusionment, the third-rate copies of Italian fashion or American entertainment. Empty bottles and plastic bags littering the riverside. The thoughtlessness in treating the environment, no longer sure it will continue to exist, no longer worth the trouble of maintaining.

Everything has become temporary, insecure, cheaply built, waiting for the next avalanche. Walking around Mostar, twenty years after that first visit, I felt no determination in the air, no confidence. Not a glimmer of the hope with which Bogdanović, whatever doubts he had about the society he was contributing to, had designed and built his monuments.

Another thing nobody expected was that a young Mostarka, whose father was imprisoned during the war and who fled with her family to the Netherlands, would one day return as an architect with a passion for public space, and with a style of design that is stern and inclusive, that listens to the stories the city has kept to itself for so long, that allows spaces to build their own understanding.

Mortal Cities
Forgotten Monuments

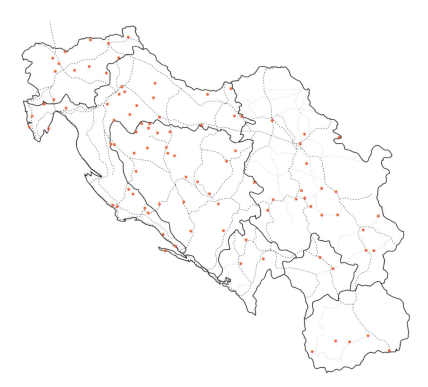

All monuments in former Yugoslavia commemorating the Second World War.

The conqueror, the conquered, and the indestructible joy of life

---

Former Yugoslavia, the country where the First World War began, has always been a breeding ground for conflict. Due to its geographical location between Western and Eastern Europe, many powers, both before and after the First World War, had an interest in conquering this region, and borders shifted continuously. Bosnians, Serbs, and Croats, as well as minority groups like Roma and Jews were consecutively ruled by the Ottomans and the Austrian Empire. These confrontations resulted in a mix of different cultures and religions, and a wide variety of cultural remnants and heritage from these different periods. All these different groups imagined and legitimized their identities in reference to particular periods, events, and individuals in their shared and mixed histories. After the Second World War ended, Yugoslavia was in ruins. Josip Broz, better known as Tito, who fought Fascism with his Partisan army, became the famous leader of the country that by then comprised six socialist republics: Slovenia, Croatia, Bosnia-Herzegovina, Serbia, Montenegro, and Macedonia. In addition, it included two autonomous provinces within Serbia: Kosovo and Vojvodina. To counter fascist and nationalist sentiments among the inhabitants of these republics and provinces, Tito introduced a strict socialist regime that continuously emphasized similarities and mutual dependency among the different people living in these different areas. After the Second World War, Yugoslavia became a laboratory for experiments on bringing together people from different backgrounds and religions into one and the same nation: not only through education, media, theater, and film, but also in architecture.

In fact, architecture played an essential role at many different turning points in the history of this area, both in the decades after the Second World War, as well as during and after the Bosnian War (1992–1995). Symbolism was of great importance during these events: not only by strategically placing particular buildings in public space, but also by deliberately destroying or avoiding specific architectural targets. From 1960 to 1980, Tito commissioned more than 100 monuments to commemorate the victims of fascism. Remarkably, these monuments did not recall the Second World War, but instead were mostly oriented toward a shared future. This future was imagined as a world of freedom, equality, independence, and progress, offering a better life for everyone—a future that could only exist due to the fact that others had sacrificed their lives. In order for the monuments to appeal to all the different inhabitants, regardless of the republic they were

Bird's eye view of Mostar after the second siege, 1994.

Bird's eye view of Vukovar after the second siege, 1994.

Garavice Memorial Park in Bihać, Bosnia-Herzegovina.

Partisan Necropolis in Mostar, Bosnia-Herzegovina.

living in or their religion, a new formal language had to be invented. This resulted in a design language that was—unlike the majority of monuments commemorating victims of war in other parts of the world—intended to be free from symbols referring to victory, war heroes and military figures, killed civilians, religion, and nationalism. Instead, abstract forms had to refer to 'the modern future'. In a country with an endless variety of cultures, ethnicities, identities, and truths, these monuments, regardless of their location, were intended to appeal to any Yugoslavian. It was hoped that a monument in Serbia could belong just as much to a Croat, Kosovar, or Bosnian as it did to a Serb. The monuments parted with history: a history steeped in tensions and shifting borders.

The monuments, often located in parks, forests, or on hills, were designed by recognized sculptors like Miodrag Živković, Jordan and Iskra Grabul, Dušan Džamonja, Vojin Bakić, and architects including Bogdan Bogdanović. Often these monuments became public spaces, where people hiked, sat down, and could spend their leisure time. Schools would organize student excursions to

these monuments,
where they learned
about the recent history
of the Second Word War,
which was presented as a new
beginning for Yugoslavia. The
most important lesson taught to
the visitors of the monuments was that
their comfortable life in Yugoslavia was only
possible thanks to the battles that the warriors
against fascism had fought in that very area. This
derived from the conviction that unity could only
be created when people imagined a common future.

Many of the monuments built after the Second World War still
exist. The monuments are predominantly located in areas where
the fiercest battles against fascism had taken place. They have
different forms, but all function in the same way. In October
2013, I visited eight of these monuments. It was a special
experience, because of the mystical nature of the
locations. Both their locations and the routes
leading to the monuments were carefully chosen
and designed. In many cases, the monuments
suddenly emerge from the landscape,
without many clues announcing
their presence. The paths to the
monuments are tortuous and the
landscape design is constantly
changing. The paths at first
often lead away from
the monument, and

Necropolis for the victims of fascism in Novi Travnik,
Bosnia-Herzegovina.

Memorial Ilirska Bistrica, Slovenia.

Makljen memorial, Bosnia-Herzegovina.

towards the end swiftly take a sharp turn towards them. Upon arrival, the site feels like an entirely new, surreal, and at the same time ancient location—an environment where one loses contact with the everyday world. The monuments—both those in the city and ones located in nature—can be experienced in different ways, as each monument employs design choices that have a connection with the specific location and the events that have happened at the spot. As a result, every visitor experiences the monuments in his or her own way, depending on their connection with the location or with historical events. Because of this, the monuments did not have the same meaning for different Yugoslavian citizens. It is likely that the citizens and soldiers who had collaborated with the Fascists during the war would feel humiliated by these monuments, as they were mostly built on the battle grounds on which Tito's Partisan armies had been victorious. However, while this recent history of defeating the shared enemy of fascism was glorified at schools and in the many films that were made about the Second

World War, marking a new start for the Socialist Federal Republic of Yugoslavia, it was not explicitly visualized by the monuments.

Due to their locations, use of material, construction method, and sheer size, the monuments have proved to be almost impossible to destroy, which is why a large number of them could not be demolished during the Yugoslavian Civil War in the 1990s. However, because of this war, the status and meanings of the monuments have shifted. The majority of them are either damaged or left to the effects of nature. The monuments can now be considered as tombstones that are reminiscent of the land that once used to be called Yugoslavia. Some of the monuments are located in cities that for the most part were destroyed during the Civil War and are nowadays ethnically divided, such as Mostar (Bosnia-Herzegovina) and Vukovar (Croatia).

The architect who designed many of the monuments ordered by Tito was the architect and urban planner Bogdan Bogdanović. Like the other monuments, those

Kosmaj monument on the Kosmaj mountain in Serbia.

designed
by   Bogdanović   lack
any symbolism of political ideology,
war heroes, or religion. Nevertheless, his
monuments are exceptions in comparison to the
abstract formal language that most of the others employ.
Especially in the early days of his career as a monument
designer, Bogdanović used a formal language with references
to old mythology, and the Renaissance and Baroque periods. Due
to this, many of his monuments do not refer to a 'modern' future
as the other monuments do, such as for example the Battle of
Sutjeska memorial in Tjentište, which was designed by Miodrag
Živković. What can we learn from the design language employed
by Bogdanović? In contrast to those 'modern' monuments, those
designed by Bogdanović appear to be ancient and look like they
will be there eternally. In his book *Grad i smrt (City and death)*,
Bogdanović explains: "I chose non-ethnic and non-confessional
symbols, trying to stay as far away from ideo-political symbols. I
often sought inspiration in archaeological materials; I ventured
deeper into the world of archaic images; I was looking for ancient
imaginative matrices. I wanted, in terms of the universal human,
the presumed 'anthropological memories', to represent war
and death, the conqueror, the conquered, and above all the
indestructible joy of life."[1] Bogdanović always tried to express one
of the elements—fire, water, earth and air—within his monuments.
Most of the monuments he designed were site-specific and used
the spatial qualities and materials of the direct environment.

What is special about these monuments is that they never
represented the present or the recent past, but always referred
to a distant past to imagine a future or—as is the case with

the monuments by Bogdan Bogdanović—eternity. Currently, the demolished cities like Mostar and Vukovar employ architecture as a continuation of the battle instead of a means to rebuild the city after the battles. Nowadays, the old monuments that are located within these destroyed cities are one of the few places where one can 'read' the historical traces of the city and therefore offer social and historical reflection. Based on this, one can choose for oneself in which way to relate to this history. This is very much needed, especially in destroyed cities where many places are burdened with tensions, and where truths and meanings are imposed upon their inhabitants. Nowadays, these cities do not have any places where both culture and society are represented, contested, challenged, and turned upside down. Keeping and preserving architectural remnants from a different political period reminds us of the diversity of politics and history. A varied visual frame of reference may allow citizens to see both current and historical politics in a broader perspective, resulting in a more tolerant and inclusive approach towards each other. Therefore, the monuments can fulfill an important role in the destroyed cities and may even be more important than the role these monuments used to have in the past.

42

Tjentište,
Bosnia and Herzegovina
43° 20′ 54.00″ N,
18° 41′ 26.00″ E

44

Bihać, Bosnia and
Herzegovina
44° 49′ 0.00″ N,
15° 52′ 0.00″ E

Mostar, Bosnia and Herzegovina
43° 20′ 32.18″ N,
17° 48′ 45.91″ E

Jasenovac,
Croatia
45° 16' 14.61" N,
16° 54' 41.08" E

Vukovar,
Croatia
45° 20′ 42.86″ N,
19° 0′ 3.67″ E

Belgrade,
Serbia
44o48'42.74"N
20o29'06.12" O

Čačak,
Serbia
43° 52′ 60.00″ N,
20° 21′ 0.00″ E

Popina,
Serbia
43° 35' 49.00'' N,
20° 56' 59.00'' E

"Cities often exist for centuries. Languages and nations are often shorter-lived—generations pass through, foreign peoples, new rulers, a multitude of languages, the city survives it all."

Chris Keulemans in *Van de zomer naar de werkelijkheid.*

The unwritten rules
of the urban environment

Architecture has a strong influence on people's feelings and their daily lives as these fixed points of reference are fundamental to their sense of space. Each of us is very attached, either consciously or unconsciously, to certain buildings, streets, or squares in our environment. Often, it is presumed that the city we live in will always be there. We often simply assume that the offices in which we work, the school buildings where we are taught, the supermarkets where we do our groceries, and the buildings we live in will never disappear. Likewise, it is hard to imagine that monuments that were built to last will ever be gone. It might be possible for city dwellers to imagine moving to a different city, or that certain buildings receive different functions, or might be replaced by new ones. But it is hard to imagine losing a city or to envision the buildings in a city disappearing or being transformed into ruins. Unsurprisingly, people are emotionally traumatized when their cities are destroyed: they lose their physical point of reference. This is exactly what happened in Mostar: not a single inhabitant would ever have thought that their city would be annihilated and that only a specter of what their city once was would remain.

Architecture not only played a major role in the former Yugoslavia in the decades after the Second World War, but also during and after the war in Bosnia-Herzegovina (1992-1995). I will focus on the city of Mostar when describing this role, because of its high personal significance to me. In September 1993, in the midst of the Civil War, I fled Bosnia-Herzegovina together with my parents. In the summer of 1999, we came back to visit the country for the first time. During that summer, and the many summers that would follow, we visited cities like Sarajevo and Mostar. Full of wonder, I studied the demolished cities and buildings. For me, it was, and still is, a unique, but unsettling experience to visit a city in such a condition.

The Old Bridge built in Ottoman style in 1566.
The Gymnasium in Moorish revival style in 1902.

Mostar used to be the paragon of tolerance and was known as the city with the most mixed marriages in former Yugoslavia. Before the war, no one wondered whether his or her neighbor was Orthodox, Muslim, or Catholic. Founded in the thirteenth century, the city has a rich Ottoman, Austro-Hungarian, and Yugoslavian history. The inhabitants of Mostar therefore expressed varying ways of relating to identity and religion, depending on the particular politics of a certain period. Historically, the citizens of Bosnia-Herzegovina have been divided into three groups based on their religious background: Catholicism, Eastern Orthodox Christianity, and Islam. Names and surnames may reveal which background you have, or your parents or grandparents. Depending on the ruling power, one of the religious minorities would gain power and grow into a majority. At times, when feelings of nationalism grew stronger, which was for example the case during the First and Second World Wars, Catholics in Bosnia would consider themselves to be part of Croatia, while the Orthodox Christians would affiliate themselves with the Serbian nation and the (Muslim) Bosnians would cultivate their nationalist feelings for Bosnia.

However, during the Socialist Federal Republic of Yugoslavia, under the rule of Tito, nationalism and religion was suppressed and became a decreasingly important issue. Instead, most people increasingly identified themselves with being Yugoslavian, for which 'unity and fraternity' was an important motto. In this way, it was possible for the different groups of people to live together quietly under this regime. Catholic Croats or Orthodox Serbs living in the Bosnian Republic would consider themselves as belonging to the country of Yugoslavia. In other words: everyone was part of the same country and had the same passport. Moreover, a Yugoslav passport was even a widely sought-after document, as it allowed its owner to travel freely all over the world. Tito succeeded in uniting all the different inhabitants of the republics of Yugoslavia, but this sudden feeling of unity was not surprising, as the inhabitants shared culture, history, territory, language, and many other traditions. They also largely shared the idea and the will to be part of the same people: to be Yugoslavian. During most of the existence

of the Socialist Federal Republic of Yugoslavia, many people did not profess a religion: being a Catholic, Orthodox Christian, or Muslim was to many inhabitants some kind of formality, which simply signified your ancestor's religion. Religious festivities including Christmas, Eid al-Fitr (Sugar Feast), or one's name day would be celebrated together.

True City Dwellers

In Mostar, various groups of people lived peacefully together and historical influences from a variety of cultures were clearly visible in the architecture of these cities. Architectural historian Emily Gunzburger Makaš describes how most tourist guidebooks displayed the prewar physical city as a place that made visible how "different cultures meet [and] interweave", or as a "kaleidoscope of oriental, Byzantine, pseudo-Moorish and western elements"[2]. Another important asset of the identity of Mostar was the Old Bridge, symbolizing the connection between and tolerance among different people, cultures, and periods. It was not only an important symbol for the city of Mostar and the whole country, but most of all an important public space where people got together. It was a meeting place; for generations, it was a spot where couples would plan their first date and where the famous annual diving competitions were held. It did not matter what your religion or background was. One simply was a Mostarac or Mostarka.

Modern high rise buildings in Mostar built in the 1960's.

Religion and nationalism were largely insignificant under the rule of Tito. Instead, it was important to meet the traits and codes of conduct that

belong to living in a city and urban life, which were put to the test in public life. Bogdan Bogdanović reflected upon this by stating: "Urbanity is one of the highest abstractions of the human spirit. To me, to be an urban man means to be neither a Serb nor a Croat, and instead to behave as though these distinctions no longer matter, as if they stopped at the gates of the city." In order to achieve this, all inhabitants of a city have to once again "learn how to read the city." If we cannot read the city, we can never reach a higher level: "the art of writing a city."
In other words, if we don't understand the physical structures and their different historical layers that surround us, we will never know how to use these public spaces and how to insert new meaning into them; how to live together, how to build and rebuild and how to give room for appropriation.
Mostar has traditionally always been a very social city in which public activities, such as 'promenading' along the Korzo, the public street cabaret (Liskaluk), and diving off the Old Bridge were all very important premises for the city to function.

Promenading was an urban activity that belonged to all inhabitants of Mostar, and many other cities in former Yugoslavia. The street that would be promenaded on was called the Korzo. Between six and ten in the evenings was a time of seeing and of being seen, catching up with people, and laughing and flirting. In Mostar, the Korzo was the road that led from the old Hit department store, via the Gymnasium and Tito's Bridge, towards the Razvitak department store.
In Mostar, an important part of the Korzo used to be the nightly gathering in bars to witness the Mostar Liskaluk. This is a particular kind of cabaret, consisting of witty and funny responses to urban topics. The performers were called Liske. These would not be professional comedians, but regular citizens of Mostar who had a day job. At night, they would gather in the bars to recite the jokes they just thought of. Before the war, they often would come together in the Bristol and

Neretva hotels.
Another important tradition of Mostar is diving off of the Old Bridge, which has occurred since 1567. It used to be a ritual where young men dove off the bridge to prove their manliness and impress young women. Later it became a tradition that was carried on from one generation of Mostar men to the next. Boys learned step by step how to dive, and ultimately become skilled enough to jump off the Old Bridge. A diving contest is held every year, where both locals as well as the most famous international high board divers take the plunge.

Public squares, parks, and boulevards were the stage where citizens would display these urban activities. Being a city dweller is what connects the inhabitants of Mostar to each other. A city dweller is somebody who can adapt to the unwritten rules of the urban environment; being civilized used to be very important in Mostar before the last war. If you were, you would belong to the Raja and deserved the title of Raja. Roko Markovina, who was elected as the most beloved Mostarian on multiple occasions and is currently a professor at the Faculty of Electrical Engineering, Mechanical Engineering and Naval Architecture at the University of Split, Croatia, describes this as follows:
"The real 'divide' in Mostar, during my childhood, youth, and still now as an adult, could be

traced back to one single division: either you were a member of the Raja and their codes of conduct, or you belonged to the papak (a person who is not adapted to the urban way of living—somebody without manners) or even worse: to the đubrad (bastards). This is the only true division, at least as far as I'm concerned, and still the most honest and most correct one, because of the simple reason that it disqualifies any national, religious, sexual, racial, cultural, or intellectual differences. If you were OK, you were Raja, if you weren't, you were a papak or đubrad! And that's all there is to it. This moral fitness and the belonging to one of the three categories was decided by the Raja, the čaršija (the Old City), and the people in it. Accurate to the millimeter and [...] infallible. You would carry the title that was appointed to you by the Raja or čaršija with you for your entire life until your death. You could only receive your title once, and only lose it once. Second chances did not exist for the Raja. It was very hard for a papak or đubrad to become a Raja, because the classification was made according to one's character and certain moral traits. Only once these most important, I would say 'primary', differences were considered, certain other 'secondary differences' could be considered— although these would still not mean very much to the Raja. These could be differences in religion, culture, tradition, habits, language, and dialect, perhaps in manners, appearance and look, erudition, knowledge, or cooking skills. Other, more important 'differences' simply did not exist, and I certainly haven't known any other in my life. I'll be honest: we did not take it into account whatsoever. This type of diversity is a treasure for every multiethnic and multinational environment, especially for a city the way Mostar used to be. I say used to be until 1990, because nowadays Mostar is no longer like this.

"Raja! What a beautiful sounding word! The only word that is capable of describing the whole of life. A word that cannot even be defined in an entire novel. Raja [...] it's an attitude towards life, it is a philosophy, principles you would betray even when your own life is in danger; it's security, morality, friendship. Whether you could belong to the Raja did not depend on your nationality, religion, wealth, poverty, intelligence, profession, first name, or family name. The most valuable trait one could posses in order to be a member of Raja was one's character. Something similar to this is called ekipa in Split, škvadra in Rijeka, klapa in Dalmatia and dečki in Zagreb. But nowhere was this as meaningful as being a Raja in Mostar.

"Although the origins of the word are completely different (servants, the enslaved, repressed and humiliated—people without rights), in the city, is simply meant that such a person was 'real'. It meant that people could count on you, that you would not be a headache to any other person in the Raja, that you would not betray anyone, and that others could trust that you would think the same of them. It meant you will never be fooled, that you are no šupak, that you cannot stand papke, that you will never use people as a means for something, or would do something foolish on purpose. Raja is synonymous with a good person, a friend or somebody close to you; synonymous with an honest, dependable person, with a 'real player', devoted to the general idea of the good, a person who, even in the hardest of times, doesn't give in. You could not just get your membership to the Raja, especially not with money. Being a part of the Raja was not something that could be bought. You simply had or hadn't deserved it thanks to your personal character and values.

"A variety of different people would belong to one and the same Raja: intellectuals (doctors, engineers, professors, lawyers, economists, musicians), but also craftsmen, homeless people, 'smugglers' (hustlers)—every profession that would require some qualities and worked according to the codes of conduct of the Raja. "There was a lot of mutual respect and people always helped each other. To this day, there still is a lot of respect for one another. People have lived by the codes of conduct without exception. Even the poorest, who had to live off hustling and resale. As far as I remember, it never occurred that a smuggler would charge somebody of the Raja more for a pair of jeans or a cinema ticket than the purchase price.

"Raja was a noble, human, and solitary group of people, with the only (very minor) defect being that, during certain events, some would have a bit too much to drink. However, this deficiency—often caused by heartbreak—was compensated by other virtues, so they would stay beloved anyway. Raja were esteemed people, because they were positive, progressive, spontaneous, and informal. They were always surrounded by friends, which meant a great deal to them throughout their whole lives.

"Becoming Raja was hard. Once you were one, you had certain rights, but even more responsibilities—and they were not to be neglected. You had to be willing to carry this 'load' for the rest of your life, which is not easy. You could only become Raja once. If you lost this honor, you would not be able to regain it. Some, who were Raja, had forgotten this during the war, and they subsequently lost their titles. They had violated the unwritten but well-known codes of conduct, and now they are nobody and nothing as far as the Raja's concerned. Raja knows what has happened… and remembers it.

"One more thing: Raja was not able to hate. Raja either loved, or was indifferent. If Raja was indifferent towards you, it was worse than if they hated you—hate is a sign of love as well, just with a negative undercurrent, and it at least would mean that you exist, that you are being noticed. But when somebody is indifferent to you, it means you're not there. You simply do not exist."[3] The codes of conduct of Raja disappeared after the war. A commonly shared etiquette of the 'city dweller' no longer exists. People

still promenade to a great extent in Mostar, but nowadays it's separated: at the western (Croatian) side of the city people promenade along the King Peter Krešimir IV road (named after a king under whose reign the Croatian realm reached its territorial peak, earning him the epithet 'the Great', which is otherwise unique in Croatian history). The people of Mostar often also call it Blejićeva Street, which literally means the staring street. On the eastern (Bosnian) side of the city, people promenade on Braće Fejića Street (which after the Second World War was named after the brothers Fejić who, born and raised on this street, died as warriors in the battle against fascism). Now that a lot of the public places that used to be their stages have disappeared, the Liskaluk cabaret tradition has become a more private urban affair, taking place in theaters/bars in very small and private groups. However, it is still seen as an important part of the identity of Mostar. Diving off the Old Bridge is also a continued tradition. Despite the fact that this tradition takes place on the eastern side of the city, it has remained a shared tradition, practiced by people from all religious backgrounds. This tradition is so deeply rooted in the soul of the city that this public activity may be a perfect way to once again connect people. Urban spaces can become public and shared again by investigating local, shared urban public activities that are not bound to religion or nationalism, such as diving off the bridge, promenading and liskaluk, and by facilitating and establishing these activities through architectural interventions. In this way the persona of Raja and its urbanity can transcend differences in religion and nationalism, and urban spaces can be reclaimed as public.

When Tito passed away in 1981, the country suffered from a severe economic depression and, in the next two decades, feelings of nationalism became stronger.

After Slovenia and Croatia declared their independence from Yugoslavia in 1991, Bosnia-Herzegovina passed a referendum for independence in 1992. This was rejected by the political representatives of the Bosnian Serbs, who had established their own republic, Republika Srpska with Banja Luka as the capital. The Croats also aimed at securing parts of Bosnia-Herzegovina as Croatian and founded the Croatian Republic of Herzeg-Bosnia, with Mostar as the capital. The Serb and Croat political leadership had agreed on a partition of Bosnia with the Karađorđevo and Graz Agreements. The Bosnians however, had no share in this new distribution of territory, and fought against it. Therefore, all three groups were either defending or trying to conquer territory that they believed to be theirs. The war lasted four years and ended with the signing of the Dayton Agreement in December 1995. During these years, approximately 200,000 people were killed, hundreds of thousands more were wounded, and at least 30,000 women were raped. Half the country's population was forced to leave their homes: more than a million moved elsewhere in Bosnia and another million left the country altogether. Industrial production dropped to less than twenty percent of pre-war levels and Bosnia-Herzegovina's gross national product was a quarter of what it was in 1990. Entire villages, city centers, and monuments lay in ruins.[4]

During this war, Mostar and its inhabitants suffered severely, particularly because the city's formerly multicultural image was also lost. The city was destroyed and divided in the course of two separate battles. As described by Gunzburger Makaš, the first siege of Mostar took place in the spring of 1992 when the city was surrounded and shelled by Bosnian-Serb paramilitaries and the Army of the Serb Republic (VRS), with support from the Yugoslav People's Army (JNA). Their heavy artillery attack lasted three months and was successfully defended by the Mostar Battalion of the newly formed and poorly equipped Army of Bosnia-Herzegovina, as well as by the Bosnian-Croat militia known as the HVO. The second major siege of the city began in May 1993. This time, the city was attacked by the HVO with military and

November 9, 1993.

financial support from the Croatian Army. The HVO first cleansed the western part of the city of non-Croats. Most Muslims and the few remaining Serbs fled to the already severely damaged eastern part of Mostar, which the HVO then began shelling from previously secured positions in the hills around the city. In March 1994, the Washington Agreement put an end to the war.[5]

Mostar was the most heavily damaged city of the war in Bosnia. Ninety per cent of the center was damaged and a third of its buildings was completely destroyed. Thousands of people were killed and tens of thousands were displaced from their homes and from the city, while another ten thousand others in turn moved to Mostar. This physical and demographic change clearly affected the city's post-war climate. However, the war's most notorious legacy in Mostar is the city's political and psychological division into Croat and Muslim sides.[6] Nowadays, each area has its own schools, fire department, hospital, football team, bus station, and cellular underground network. In addition, it should be noted that other groups besides these two ethnic identities also live in Mostar. There are also people who consider themselves belonging to none of these groups, and there are people from mixed marriages who don't count themselves to one specific group. These people are spread over both parts of the city.

War against architecture

The war in Bosnia-Herzegovina can in some ways be considered to be a war against the architecture of the city. Not just by demolishing any arbitrary buildings, but by targeting specific symbolic architecture—buildings with which the inhabitants identified themselves and their culture: important cultural heritage, such as libraries, museums, universities, and squares. By destroying such significant buildings, not only a history and culture of a city are destroyed, but also the identification of the inhabitants with the city disappears.

In his book *The Destruction of Memory, Architecture at War*, the architecture critic Robert Bevan explains the logic behind a war against architecture: "Here, architecture takes on a totemic quality: a mosque, for example, is not simply a mosque; it represents to its enemies the presence of a community marked for erasure. A library or art gallery is a cache of historical memory, evidence that a given community's presence extends into the past and legitimizing it in the present and on into the future. In these circumstances, structures and places with certain meanings are selected for oblivion with deliberate intent."[7]

This is exactly what happened in Mostar. The destruction did not just affect the citizens because large parts of the city were destroyed, but because it specifically destroyed symbolic places. There was a systematic destruction of buildings of Ottoman origin, but also monuments associated with Partisans and the Second World War. Also places where the education of history and culture could take place, like libraries and schools, were destroyed deliberately. To demolish particular significant buildings is a well-known psychological warfare tactic, also according to the writer Milan Kundera. In *The Book of Laughter and Forgetting*, he describes how this kind of warfare works: "The first step in liquidating a people is to erase its memory. Destroy its books, its culture, its history. Then you have somebody write new books, manufacture a new culture, invent a new history. Before long the nation will begin to forget what it is and what is was."[8] By destroying everything the inhabitants of Mostar could identify themselves with, they became psychologically disabled. In this way people lose hope, get emotionally paralyzed, and lose their ability to fight back. Moreover, new traditions were created, particular new histories conceived, emphasized and remembered, and new monuments erected.

During the first war of Mostar in 1992, an incredible number of cultural heritage sites were deliberately destroyed in just two months. This becomes clear from *Mostar '92 Urbicid*, a book from that time, in which writer Krešimir Šego elaborates on this destruction: "All the bridges have been destroyed except the Old Bridge; out of 14 town mosques only two remained undamaged. The Catholic church at Potoci village, the Franciscan church in Mostar, the Episcopical Residence, the monastery of the Franciscan sisters at Bijelo Polje have been burnt, the Cathedral of Mostar shelled. The Palace of Culture, the museum, the archives, and the library have been damaged. All of the Mostar hotels, schools, dormitories, and colleges have been ruined. The town beauty, the hotel 'Neretva' is on fire. The 'town houses' are ablaze: the bath, the court, the Town Hall, the cadastre."[9] And this was only the beginning. During the second siege, the destruction resumed. Also the Partisan Necropolis by Bogdanović, Café Rondo, the Bristol Hotel, the Ruža Hotel, the Razvitak and Hit department stores, and the Gymnasium were heavily damaged. The more buildings got destroyed, the harder it was for the inhabitants to read and recognize the city that was engraved in their memories. Their history disappeared, and with it, the legibility of their identity, because its history is no longer visible in the traces of architecture and public space of the city. Towards the end, many people felt crushed and became increasingly apathetic, but they clung to the hope that the Old Bridge would survive. It was the only connection left between the two sides of the city. Besides this, it was the symbol of the city: an image of the connection between the two parts of the city and an emblem of tolerance and unity. The city was the bridge, and the bridge was the city. An attack on this bridge would be a violation of the concept of multi-ethnicity. If the bridge disappeared, Mostar would cease to exist since the soul of the city would be lost. As a war strategy, the attackers meticulously planned what to destroy and what not to destroy. Their aim was to psychologically incapacitate the inhabitants of the city. The psychological targets were the structures with which people identified themselves and their culture. When the façades of a city are destroyed, its face lies beyond recognition, but when its cultural, historical, and public places are targeted, it deprives the city of its legibility, disconnecting the inhabitants from their surroundings. When the bridge was ultimately destroyed, the city took its last breath. The city turned out to be mortal: the city was dead. Precisely what Bogdanović always feared the most, namely, what he called the 'ritual killing of cities', is what happened over here.

It is fascinating to think that architecture, in this case a bridge, can mean so much to the inhabitants of a city. This phenomenon is explored in *Destruction of Memory, Architecture at War*: "Why do we feel more pain looking at the image of the destroyed bridge than the image of massacred people?" Asked Croatian writer Slavenka Drakulić at the time: "Perhaps because we see our own mortality in the collapse of the bridge. We expect people to die; we count on our own lives to end. The destruction of a monument to civilization is something else. The bridge in all its beauty and grace was built to outlive us; it was an attempt to grasp eternity. It transcends our individual destiny. A dead woman is one of us—but the bridge is all of us forever."[10] In other words, when the bridge, a solid, robust, and everlasting eternal artifact, is destroyed, our shared histories and collective identities are extinguished.

Destroying symbolic architecture, both denies and erases the history and the present of the citizens of a city. Unsurprisingly, one loses all hope in such circumstances and feels displaced and uprooted. But what remains of a city when its citizens lose hope? A city then will find itself in a very dangerous condition. According to Bogdanović, destroyed cities should listen to their own memories and rebuild a new version of themselves with the old one in mind.[11] Bogdanović argues that "We all carry, even now, our eternal city within ourselves—if only because we do not know another way to structure the world around us." Architecture is a fundamental way for people to relate to their surroundings. Now that this relationship has ceased to exist, architecture is put to the task of facilitating new ways of relating to the city, without losing the soul of a city.

Destruction of Mostar during the civil war (1992–1995).

Demolished bridges of Mostar

Bridges on this page above, left to right:

1. Aviator's bridge, southern part of the city.
2. Emperor's Franz Joseph's bridge (Tito's bridge), constructed in 1882 and 1935.
3. The railway bridge at Sutina, northern part of the city, constructed in 1966.

Bridges on this page from above, left to right:

1. Hasan Brkić`s Bridge, constructed in 1980.
2. Carinski Bridge, constructed in 1918.
3. The railway bridge at Baćevići, southern part of the city, constructed in 1966.
4. The bridge at Vojno, northern outskirts.
5. Mujaga Komadina's bridge (Lucki bridge), constructed in 1913.

"All that is left of that original promise is that the former city of the dead and the former city of the living still look at each other— only now they gape with empty, black, and scalding eyes."

Bogdan Bogdanović in *Grad mojih prijatelja*

Mostar's empty stare:
1566–1966–2016

When the architect Bogdan Bogdanović witnessed the severe destruction of Mostar during the last war, he was deeply moved and struck down with fever for a couple of days. As homage to the city and to show the significance of the Partisan Necropolis, he wrote an article entitled "The City of my Friends". I will briefly introduce the history of the Partisan Necropolis, and touch upon my own experiences.

The Partisan Necropolis monument was built exactly 400 years after the famous Old Bridge of Mostar. The construction of this bridge in the 16th century in Mostar proved to be an important crowning achievement for the city. Mostar got its name from the bridge keepers, *mostari*, who would watch people from their towers entering the city via the bridge as they crossed the Neretva river ('most' means 'bridge' in Serbo-Croation). The Old Bridge, designed by the Ottoman architect Mimar Hayrudin, had become the symbol of the city. Mostar's inhabitants regarded it as an old soul that connected two parts of the city through a simple and friendly gesture. It was a symbol of the collective life of two inseparable sides: it bridged people.
A new symbol reflecting the same ideal of bridging different people was built 400 years later. The Partisan Necropolis, a monument designed in 1966 by the architect Bogdan Bogdanović, was dedicated to earth and stone. In this rocky Mediterranean city, with its tradition of carving relief onto tombstones dating back to the eleventh century, cobblestone roads, and legacy of building on top of rocks, Bogdanović designed a cemetery commemorating

810 Partisans from Mostar. He described the monument as an 'acro-necropolis' and as a microcosm of the city of Mostar where "the city of the dead mirrors the city of the living." The cemetery has the same cobblestones, alleys, and gates that are so characteristic for Mostar. Furthermore, the element of water was an important aspect of the design. It reflects the location and independence of the city situated at the Neretva river. The monument comprises five terraces through which the water flows downwards to eventually end up in a kind of niche with ribbed steps. All the way at the top, on the fifth level, is a fountain, paired with the central architectural element of the monument: a cosmological sundial.[12] During the Second World War, Mostar was known as 'the red city' because it had a particularly strong Antifascist resistance, of which its members were of Serbian, Croatian, and Muslim ethnicity. Traces of this resistance can be found on the gravestones of the Partisan Necropolis, where the different names are distributed proportionally according to the percentage of the population representing each ethnicity at the time the monument was built. The monument was a public park that marked a new, shared start after the Second World War.

2016 marks the passing of 50 years since the construction of the Partisan Necropolis. No one could have foreseen the horrors that would happen in the following 50 years. During the Civil War between 1992 and 1995, a large part of the city had been destroyed. The 'old friend' of the city, the Old Bridge, was destroyed in 1993 and resurrected in 2004. Due to

In October 2013, two sheets laid in front of the Partisan Nectropolis in Mostar, quoting Bogdan Bogdanović:

" Still we carry this immortal city within / I fear a city without memory, just as I fear people without subconsciousness.

Polis
Metropolis
Megapolis
Necropolis."

Partisan Necropolis in the 1980s.

Partisan Necropolis in 2015.

the city's current extreme segregation, the function of the bridge has disappeared: the Old Bridge no longer serves as a connection, but rather separates the city. The Partisan Necropolis was also very badly damaged during the war. Although it was restored afterwards, vandals demolished it subsequently. It seems that this place is now politically too sensitive to be demolished completely, but then again too loaded to be protected. Instead, the monument and its surroundings are largely abandoned.

Now that times have changed, the monuments remind us of the past, but at the same time reveal a lot more. At a single location, a monument can simultaneously tell something about a country, an area, a city, a battle, and a history. It is both a reflection upon society and a utopian message about the future. The monuments have the potential to address multiple nations, ethnicities, and religions (from all over the world) that would normally be irreconcilable. These monuments were intended as 'isolated' places from which peo-

---

ple could gain a positive attitude towards the future and at the same time commemorate those who died fighting fascism. Today the monuments are places that remember the time when the land where the monuments were built was once called Yugoslavia, but they also commemorate the demise of that country. For some, it evokes feelings of nostalgia for a country in a time when everything was better, and for others it represents dystopia: the Civil War of the 1990s and the collapse of Yugoslavia.

In August 2015, I visited the monument as part of my annual ritual. Every year I walk through the Old City, I cross the 'new' Old Bridge, via the Korzo (the old promenade), past the many ruins on the 'Spanish Square', by the Bruce Lee monument, along the Rondo and the old House of Culture (now House of Croats), to the Partisan Necropolis. Three years ago, it was already overgrown, neglected, and a shady hangout. Last year, I was too scared to go up into the park, the grass was too high and the entrance had been set on fire just a few months before. This time,

I wanted to try again, despite being warned of the dangers by many taxi drivers and friends from Mostar. It is supposed to be too dangerous as many visitors are threatened and called 'communists'. As I visited the monument with three friends in the middle of the day in a 40° C heat wave, we were almost sure no one else would be there. The place had been taken over by nature, littered with broken beer bottles, and the stones were daubed with nationalist and fascist writings. I have been able to accept many nationalist

---

and politically loaded decisions made with respect to public space in post-war Mostar, but the assault on the Partisan Necropolis and neglect of former Yugoslavia's most beautiful city park is upsetting.

Hopefully, "The city of my friends" by Bogdanović and the images on the next pages can convey my pain at the imminent disappearance of this unique piece of land, which is officially listed as heritage, but is in no way protected as a precious site.

Grad mojih prijatelja
(The city of my friends)

by Bogdan Bogdanović

Many of the memorial buildings to which I have devoted my mental and physical strength do not exist any more, or are, at least for now, condemned to an invisible deterioration and disappearance. I would feel miserable if—even for a moment—I allowed myself to regret, for instance, the most opulent work of my architectural youth, the Partisan Monument in Mostar, today when the real Old Mostar has long disappeared, along with the even older Mostar families, whose children lie in this honorable war cemetery. When I once explained my idea for the monument, I told a grateful audience the story of how, one day and forever after, 'two cities' would look each other in the eye: the city of dead Antifascist heroes, mostly young men and women, and the city of the living, for which they gave their lives...

It is no accident, and not without external encouragement, that this stone allegory of two cities did not end up on one of the rocky plateaus west of Mostar. The first concept probably came from a lecture I gave around the time: namely that somewhere between

heaven and earth—vaguely according to the ancient books at least—the city Hürqualyâ floats, a Sufist counterpart to the *Manichaeist Terrae lucidae*. According to gnostic speculations, this was the representation of the basis for the world's most beautiful and naïve, as well as eternally philosophical and cosmo-poetic images. And I thought that the fallen Mostar Antifascist fighters, all still boys and girls, so to speak, had the right, at least symbolically, to the beauty of dreams. The time the monument was built was a peaceful, quiet, bureaucratic time, when people had little to fear and lived in a moral environment. Looking back after twenty years of war, the purity of their motives and the all-encompassing, naive self-sacrifice can only recall the memories of the tragic crusades of our children.

Contrary to designing Jasenovac (a stone flower monument located on the site of a former concentration camp that was established by the authorities of the Independent State of Croatia during the Second World War), which was—for too many reasons—almost too difficult for me, the trips to Mostar conveyed me to a totally different world of poetry and reality. In designing the memorial in Jasenovac, the memories of the former concentration camp often placed me in a state of prolonged, nearly unbearable stress, no matter how much I tried to escape them. The construction of the Acro-Necropolis in Mostar, on the other hand, lit a deep fire within me. I endured the difficult and strenuous work without disgust or tiredness, and actually worked to channel a new perspective on life and death. Maybe it is too absurd to say so, but it was as if I hoped that I could give some of my hidden joy to my 'new friends', whose names—Muslim, Serbian,

What do stonemasons who carve a city out of space and time look like? My Mostar friends found these stonemasons on the island of Korčula in Croatia, taking everyone from the village who could hold a chisel or hammer. They were brought to Mostar at the end of the 1950s or in the early 1960s. They were modest, polite, and friendly, and they did their work religiously, almost liturgically: the resonance of their chorus-like liturgy of chiseling took five years, including a short interruption.

Partisan Necropolis and it's archaic form language.

They were lead by Barba, which means uncle and grandfather in their dialect. He was the paternal head of the fellowship, a guardian, the person who, once they returned to the island, would report to the parents and fiancées about who did what and how. Once Barba arrived, he determined a location for the 'quarry', built a construction shed, and made room for his work bench, which resembled both a chair and a pulpit. He then ordered that this chest made out of poles—though without lid or base—be filled with sand and little pieces of stone. The block of stone being carved could lie gently therein and would not be damaged during the work. Across from his working space, directly facing him, the workers put their slightly smaller chests.

Croatian names—lined up on the terraces of the necropolis. As I had promised their families, their small superterranean city would overlook the heart of Old Mostar. It also overlooked the then still existing bridge, built by the great architect Hajrudin. Once the most beautiful and daring stone bridge in the world, it was a divine act of architectural statics, in comparison to which Bogdan was just a humble builder, as one is in comparison to a supernatural manifestation.

Because of the heat in Herzegovina, they worked more often at night than during the day: from dawn until breakfast and from dusk till deep in the night. During the summer months, Mostar—that beautiful and now bygone city—and its citizens had the strong habit of waiting in the street for the coolness to emerge from the riverbed of the Neretva around midnight. Sometimes

The Partisan Necropolis was a miniature Mostar, a replica of the city on the banks of the Neretva, its ideal diagram. However, that ideogram of the city, that hieroglyph, that stone mark was not as modest in size. It had achieved the limits of a modest, primeval Balkan-Hellenic acropolis. Between the entrance—the lower gate—and the fountain at the top, one had to ascend an elevation of about twenty meters, and hike some three hundred meters of winding paths and hairpin turns. The path upwards was discernable in the splashing of the water streaming down the stone basins towards visitors.

it seemed as if everybody, even children, had forgotten that one could also sleep at night. I adopted their habit—not just because I, too, needed the coolness to get enough sleep and achieve a productive rhythm for work the following day—but also because I was playful, or rather anxious, and also even a little afraid. I had promised the inhabitants of Mostar to make something that would be unparalleled. I had driven up the costs. I had initiated a lot of work—but was I even sure that I would succeed and finish everything the way I had envisioned it?

A little feverish and distracted, I repeatedly crossed the Hajrudin's bridge from the one end of the riverbank to the other, over the cliff. Sometimes I got the idea that I was looking for advice from my predecessor about the problems he had encountered that always suddenly emerge when working with stone. I touched the stone balustrades and profiles and my fingers found things that had been obliviously overlooked during the day. In the dark, I found connections between the stones that had calcified ages ago. I felt the brackets and bonds that stopped them from shifting over the years, safeguarding the old structure from falling apart.

One night, I decided to go up to the building site. From a distance, I could hear a song, a harmony of voices, a chorus without words. Step by step, I came closer. I peered from the distance, from the darkness: acetylene lamps, or maybe even lamps from the previous century, caustic light and even more caustic shadows. In this light, something mysterious occurred. Barba—grey, hair electrified and

standing up on the back of his neck—seemed to commit a crime, like a magician, the spirit of the stones. Suddenly, he lifted the mallet and chisel up into the air, everybody lifting their hammers up in the air. They reverently kept silent. A silence took hold of the place that revealed the voices of the night—crickets, whistling nocturnal birds, the distant sound of the Neretva. One of the masons, apparently appointed for this purpose, initiated a melody without words, once again, nasal and mysterious, as in a ritual of stone worshippers. Barba picked up the rhythm with his chisel, hit the block in front of him, and started to work the stone. The song clearly prescribed the pace and force of the blow. As soon as the melody began to 'rise' (everybody was singing now), the sound of the blows became ear-splittingly loud. Once the pace 'set' again, the blows became less intense.

Every stone sounded like a musical instrument. I knew, predictably, that different kinds of stone would resonate differently—the softer the stone, the deeper the tone. It is paradoxical, and also a bit comical,

that the most solid granite whispers, that marble sings a mezzo-soprano, and chalk, the most musical stone, sings a beautiful, velvet-soft alto. Sculptors know how to perceive, and even more. "Every piece sings its own song"—says one of them, in the conviction that every piece of stone is a being in itself. But when the collective blows commence, the rhythm includes every 'stone instrument'. Suddenly, every hand movement, every posture functions so that the whole orchestra serves as its own metronome, all at the same time. And when the striking tools begin to falter—a sign that their concentration is beginning to wane—Barba, the spirit of the stone, holds up his hammer, unsatisfied. It is a sign that the work will be momentarily halted and that the blows must be harmonized from the beginning. Everybody waits for the first voice and Barba's first stroke...

The fact that it was a harmony without words got me thinking that the ancient, proto-historical version came from times when people on the island, and on the mainland, spoke another forgotten, pre-Slovenian language. Civilizations changed, languages melting, but men had stayed the same... "Why doesn't the song have words?" I once asked. The replies were simple and convincing: "They're not there, they never were!" or "That's how our ancestors used to sing it as well!"

The monument was gradually built, laboriously and carefully, by voluntary contributions. Some gifts were in kind (in natura, in which case the 'natura' was stone). There was even stone from Mostar houses that had for the most part been destroyed through decay or due to urban planning. Families gladly donated their stone buildings. Even the quiet hauling of material—the

material from the Old Town included—had a symbolic value. The stones often had centuries-old traces of smoke and calcified moss. They had 'housekeepers' (a plant species). Transmitted bits of memories or the spirit of piety from one time to another mixed with huge quantities of fresh masonry, as white as cheese.

On the highest terraces, on the inner stone walls of the 'city', in the folds of the stone walls, semi-circular niches, apsides, and buttresses were scattered in the shape of hundreds and hundreds of stone flowers. At

least partly because of the belief in the ancient suspicion of the builder-alchemist that the mason is the child of the sun and the moon and that he therefore is so exceptionally suitable—even destined—to carve heavenly phenomena, the stone flowers became deeply enmeshed in the representation of the sun, the moon, planets, constellations... A place was found somewhere for the constellation of the Great Dog, which I had never been able to discern when I looked at the skies, and even for a group of stars that does not even exist in the celestial almanac, but which I nevertheless named 'Seven Slender Cows' in my imagination. For those unfamiliar with the question, these were the *Vlašići* (referring to the Mountain Vlašići in Bosnia-Herzegovina). Eventually it turned out that the Partisan Necropolis as a whole was reminiscent of the grand astronomical constellation from which we all originate.

The lilting, heathen character of the Partisan Necropolis could not remain unnoticed. Its terraces were quickly seized by children, whose playful voices echoed in a chorus amid a stone-landscape-as-stage-set, sometimes deep into the night. The only thing I might have still hoped for was then generously granted, almost as an antic. And yet, it was in earnest as well: I was to consecrate a secret niche to the left of the entrance gate that one day would accommodate my urn. However, it now seems I will not be in the company of my friends: the gravestones have cold-bloodedly and sadistically been taken away and crushed at a stone mill. All that is left of that original promise is that the former city of the dead and the former city of the living still face each other—only now they gape with empty, black and scalding eyes.

Bogdan Bogdanović in *Mostarska Informativna Revija MM*, no. 12/13, June 1997. *Mostarska Informativna Revija MM* was a magazine founded in 1966, which was dedicated to finding ways of reconnecting the people from Mostar, wherever in they world they had fled to. The magazine covered a variety of subjects which were political, critical and sometimes aimed at raising awareness.

Partisan Necropolis in Mostar.

The forgotten monuments
of former Yugoslavia

Kozara, Bosnia-Herzegovina

Knin, Croatia

Kijevo, Croatia

Jajinci, Serbia

Ploče, Croatia

Popina, Serbia

Bogdan Bogdanović

Priština, Kosovo

Petrova Gora, Croatia

Banja Luka, Bosnia-Herzegovina

Sanski Most, Bosnia-Herzegovina

Gevgelija, Republic of Macedonia

Grmeč, Bosnia-Herzegovina

Ostra, Serbia

Bosanski Novi, Bosnia-Herzegovina

Temerin, Serbia

Kadinjača, Serbia

Kosmaj, Serbia

Priština, Kosovo

Struga, Republic of Macedonia

Kavadarci, Republic of Macedonia

Šibenik, Croatia

Kruševac, Serbia

Tjentište, Bosnia-Herzegovina

Kosmaj, Serbia

Kruševo, Republic of Macedonia

Mostar, Bosnia-Herzegovina
Bogdan Bogdanović

Jelovice, Croatia

Kolašin, Montenegro

Nikšić, Montenegro

Kosovska Mitrovica, Kosovo
Bogdan Bogdanović

Slabinja, Croatia

Trvanik, Bosnia-Herzegovina
Bogdan Bogdanović

Sisak, Croatia

Kamenska, Croatia

Vlasotince, Serbia

Bogdan Bogdanović

Zagreb, Croatia

Podgora, Croatia

Sinj, Croatia

Štuti, Croata

Zagreb, Croatia

Makljen, Bosnia-Herzegovina

Belgrade, Serbia

Bogdan Bogdanović

Labin, Croatia

Bogdan Bogdanović

Čačak, Serbia

Bogdan Bogdanović

Žabljak, Montenegro

Vodice, Croatia

Zlatibor, Serbia

Podgarić, Croatia

Kragujevac, Serbia

Kragujevac, Serbia

Bihać, Bosnia-Herzegovina

Bogdan Bogdanović

Zenica, Bosnia-Herzegovina

Kruševac, Serbia

Bogdan Bogdanović

Leskovac, Serbia

Bogdan Bogdanović

Maribor, Slovenia

Prilep, Republic of Macedonia

Podsreda, Slovenia

Jezerski Vrh, Slovenia

Invisible ruins
by Thomas A. P. van Leeuwen

A ruin is a work of architecture in a state of extreme decay. While a ruin has a physical presence, its significance or meaning is usually metaphysical. The ruin itself is often not that interesting. The interesting part is the part that has disappeared, through time or through force. The ruin is there, but what it represented is absent. In fact, the absent is more present than the present. Of Pompeii, the most absent of all cities, Sigmund Freud wrote: "What had formerly been the city of Pompeii assumed an entirely changed appearance, but not a living one; it now appeared rather to become completely petrified in dead immobility. Yet out of it stirred a feeling that death was beginning to talk."[13] What is not there (anymore) speaks much louder to us and is all the more present. By leaving out most, most is left over.

Still, the problem of being affected by looking at ruins is that one has to know what it was that was ruined. On the other hand, one is better equipped to do the imagining if one knows less of what was ruined. The less one knows, the more one's imagination has to work. Indeed, there is a lot of imagining to do before the ruin starts to talk. Seventeenth and early eighteenth century explorers of the wonders of antiquity were experts in imagination. The amazing Athanasius Kircher was the undisputed master of speculative reconstruction. The ruins of Babylon, Assyria, and Egypt became worlds of unlimited interpretations. Foreign cultures, religions, and languages could be explained with marvelous results and with the help of relatively little knowledge. The Age of Enlightenment, although much better informed, was still irresistibly attracted to what it could not see: the unknown worlds of underground Rome. Centuries of destruction and neglect had heaped up billions of tons of soil and waste over the once so magnificent imperial city. Giovanni Battista Piranesi, artist, architect, and the greatest of imaginers, could have seen no more than a roofscape of quasi-sunken buildings. The Forum Romanum was a grazing ground for shepherds and their flocks and a bidonville for vagabonds. Triumphal arches stuck their heads out of the rubble as if they had just survived a massive mudslide, and temples of which only their capitals and architraves were visible served as fancy façades for cart sheds. In the *Vedute di Roma*, Piranesi had little else to record than the tips of colossal shipwrecks. Nowhere could this be better illustrated than in the closely observed remains of the Temple of Jupiter Tonans. Colossal capitals, parts of a frieze, and a segment of a fronton stick out of the ground. They are merely the upper parts of a structure that might just be ten times as big. Still, even these isolated parts exercize such a massive presence that they obscure the urban village that seems to shelter in its shadow. How much shadow would it have thrown if the complete temple had stood there?

The charm and success of Piranesi's prints was that they not only caused wonder and amazement, but also an appetite for more. Who would not have wanted to turn over the leaf, to see whether there, on the other side, the hidden rest was represented? About the same time the *Vedute* were published, Piranesi came out with what could be interpreted as the solution: the *Carceri d'invenzione*, dark nightscapes of the underworld. Traditionally the *Carceri* were interpreted as nightmarish constructions of the mind, the often quoted incarcerated souls, dark prisons inhabited by spooky creatures of the night. The *Carceri* are certainly lugubrious, but they are also manifestly tectonic, with their stocky walls, arches, and domes, desperately keeping up the immense weight of the giant buildings of which only the tops had been visible. The *Carceri* are the unlit, verso-sides of the sunny Arcadian townscapes of the *Vedute*. As architectural reconstructions of a lost substructure, they are very much in the same vein as the numerous contemporary reconstructions of another lost world, that of the fossilized world of prehistory.
Think of the public shock the bones of the mastodon produced in 1801, when the Philadelphia polymath Charles Wilson Peale showed them to the curious spectators, or by the *Tyrannosaurus rex* unearthed in 1990 in the Black Hills of South Dakota. The fossilized remains of a dinosaur are a ruin; a dead dog is not.

Pronao del Tempio della Concordia, Vedute di Roma, 1741.

Veduta del Tempio di Giove Tonante, Vedute di Roma, 1750-1758.

Ruins are about size. The ruins of Palmyra were an indication of their original dimensions; the remains of the temples of Rome inspired the imagination. Piranesi's view of the capitals of the Temple of Jupiter suggest that, from underneath the pile of ash, the temple appeared to emerge from boiling molten lava. Nero's head, a leftover of the colossal statue after which the Colosseum was named, gave an impression of the gigantic scale of the theater. The largest building ever to have become a ruin was the New York World Trade Center. The memorial's gargantuan size and brutal 'ugliness' contributed largely to its association as 'beautiful horror'.[14]

The sublime force of the 'tip of the iceberg' technique was of course not Piranesi's privilege. Etienne-Louis Boullée, a master in the representation of the architecture of horror, sketched the top of a blunt-tipped pyramid, a cenotaph, just barely visible in a stormy apocalyptic landscape, and called it 'architecture ensévelie', a buried building.

Etienne-Louis Boullée, *Architecture ensévelie.*

The horror is double: not only is the building engulfed by the Earth, but judging by the angle of the top, it must also be unbelievably big. A pyramid as large as the globe itself.

The Dudik Memorial in Vukovar, Croatia, by Bogdan Bogdanović, created between 1978-1980, is a remarkable member of the family of buried buildings. First of all, it was designed as a sunken landscape of towers, which in the years of the Civil War was moderately damaged, producing the image of a 'double ruin'. A ruin falling twice into ruin is sublimity at its best, yet not exceptional. It takes time to decay more than once, and it happens to almost all of the most ancient and most famous of ruins. The Flavian Amphitheater, or Colosseum, is in the very center of Rome. Its shape and plan are reminiscent of a belly button in their concentration. It has been desolated by disasters both man-made and natural. Its encrustation and patina of ruin has been the work of earthquakes, pillaging, vandalism, and simply of aging. After mediaeval neglect, this ancient ruin of idolatrous bloodshed was later turned into a monument to Christian martyrdom. After which, when Rome was a frequent destination for artists and travelers of the Grand Tour, they saw the Colosseum as it was then: a stone thicket of broken pillars roughly forming an oval ring of rubble. Stefano della Bella sketched this former treasure of Imperial Rome as a picturesque heap of abandoned wreckage. Then, in the 1870s, when Rome had become the capital of the new state of Italy, all the rubble and waste had to be removed; the monument was to be made presentable. Archaeologists came in and started to excavate everything that was not authentic. While doing so, the underlying sewer system came to the surface and flooding was the result. For years afterward, the Colosseum fell into another phase of ruin, this time: hydraulic collapse.[15]

Often the question arises whether we should restore ruined buildings back to their original state, even if their original state was a ruin, or should leave them as they are? Ruins tell stories in ways that are quite different from stories told by restorations. The story told by a ruin is as incomplete as the ruin itself: it has a beginning, but no end. A restoration, on the other hand, has no story but merely an end, which is, invariably, a happy end. John Ruskin's *Lamp of Memory* of 1854 is the basic condemnation of the idea of restoration. "Without architecture", Ruskin said, "we cannot remember". But architecture should remain as it was and still is. Restoration is 'a lie', that will lead to "the most total destruction, which a building can suffer: a destruction out of which no remnants can be gathered, a destruction accompanied with a false description of the thing destroyed. Do not let us deceive ourselves in this important matter; it is impossible, as impossible to raise the dead (…)."[16] In this way, the triumphalist Freedom Tower on the site of the collapsed World Trade Center Towers was a false description, a happy-end with no story to tell. Since Bogdanović's Dudik Memorial Park was ravaged during the Battle of Vukovar in 1991, no efforts were made to patch up the damaged towers. The fact that for a while the site harbored a soccer field is perhaps not a story, but an anecdote that teaches us well enough that life has to go on, even on the edge of a volcano.

Was Bogdanović inspired by Piranesi? Of course he was. Who does not know the *Vedute or the Carceri*? Great artists like Bogdan Bogdanović know their business inside out. In any case, in 1989 for the Dudik Memorial Park, Bogdanović received the first of a series of much-coveted awards. The ceremony took place in the Croatian coastal city of Piran, and as the accompanying text explained: "The award is named after the eighteenth century Italian artist and architect Giovanni Battista Piranesi (1720-1778), whose family comes from Piran."

Stefano della Bella, *Vedute Romane*, View of the Arch of Constantine,
1656 with Colosseum in the background, etching.

The irreversible
disappearance of a city

Reconstructing a new image
for Mostar

After the war, the recovery of Mostar became a slow, complex process,
partly due to the fact that the city was divided into two parts, each
belonging exclusively to one specific ethnic group.

Many of the destroyed buildings were approached in different ways
during the rebuilding process. The monument built by Bogdanović was
rebuilt with support from the Dutch and Norwegian governments and
subsequently became the target of heavy vandalism. A monument to
Croatian Defense Forces has replaced the ruins of what was once
Café Rondo. Hotel Neretva and the Razvitak department stores still lie
in ruins. The Bristol Hotel, the Gymnasium, and the Palace of Culture
have been rebuilt exactly as they were—even though the Palace of
Culture was renamed the 'Palace of Croatians'—and the site of the
ruin of the Ruža Hotel is currently being rebuilt.

In 2004, after several different support bridges and a long reconstruction
period, the Old Bridge was finally reconstructed as it looked before
the war. A year later the bridge was designated as UNESCO World
Heritage. The opening of the bridge in 2004 was world news: "In
searing heat of more than 40° C this afternoon, princes, presidents,
and prime ministers from all over Europe and the Middle East are
to attend the opening of the 'new Old Bridge,' whose restoration is
being hailed as the start of a happier new era for Mostar."[17] There was
a great celebration; trained divers jumped off the bridge with torches.

The bridge became a national and international showpiece that needed to express it had once again succeeded in unifying the two different ethnic groups of Mostar. If this were possible in Mostar—the city with the most complex political situation of all—it would be possible in all of Bosnia-Herzegovina. At the UNESCO website, one can read that "the reconstructed Old Bridge and old city of Mostar are symbols of reconciliation, international collaboration and the peaceful coexistence of different cultural, ethnic, and religious communities".[18]

For the construction of the new Old Bridge, stones were used that had been quarried from exactly the same mountain as centuries ago, and it was rebuilt using the same technique. Besides reconstructing the Old Bridge, the area in close proximity to the bridge was also restored, made into more or less of a copy of the way it was before the war. While this restoration was executed with a lot of care and precision, the bridge turned out whiter and smoother than the way the Mostarci and Mostarke remembered. Although some old pieces of the original bridge now lie at the pebble beach and serve as places to sit, the entire site does not reveal any of its recent history. The demolition of the Old Bridge was to many inhabitants of Mostar a symbol of the annihilation of the city, which is denied by the new version. Copying the bridge at another moment in time suggests the intention of wanting to erase the entire era of the war and taking a leap backwards in time. However, by creating a historical copy and inserting it into the present, the bridge's users will only remain at a distance, as they will be unable to relate to it, because it is not an 'honest' approach to its recent history.

Rebuilding the Old Bridge seems to have been first and foremost a way for international organizations and governments, which had been involved in reconstructing Bosnia-Herzegovina for years, to show their

Foto: Studio HADŽIĆ Mostar   juli/july 1992

Foto: Studio HADŽIĆ Mostar

avgust/august 1993

success and gradually waive their responsibilities in this process. Media all over the world covered the reconstruction of the Old Bridge, and therefore it became a media phenomenon signifying the reconstruction of an image rather than a true and enduring restoration of the social function of this piece of architecture and public space. I wish that UNESCO's optimism were justified, but the actual situation in the city is completely the opposite. In many respects, the rebuilding of the Old Bridge was a positive event since many of Mostar's inhabitants were proud at the opening ceremony and it was an event that for once had Bosnia in the international news in a positive way. However, the new Old Bridge nonetheless gained a different meaning. It simply is, both physically and psychologically, not the same bridge to the current and former inhabitants of Mostar. The symbolic meaning of the bridge attributed by the international media and UNESCO among others, namely, as connecting the "two divided parts of Mostar", is incorrect, as the Old Bridge and the old center are in the area that was allocated after the war to the Muslim Bosnians. Another problem is the Ottoman history of the old city, which has been overly emphasized after the restoration, but which is, unsurprisingly, associated with Islamic culture by the Croats in Mostar. Moreover, references to Ottoman history are also being exploited as the authentic oriental history of the city for tourists, which is continuously emphasized by the many souvenir shops selling 'oriental' products and cafés that don't serve alcohol. This development may have instigated economic profits for the citizens that work in the tourist industry, but are in no way beneficial for creating a public space that is able to bring together both Croats and Muslims. The original function of the bridge was simple: to get people from one side of the city to the other, using the bridge as an infrastructural tool instead of linking it to only one part of history or one identity. Crossing this bridge is nowadays mainly done by tourists, of whom some might not have the slightest clue of its history and are

Foto: Studio HADŽIĆ Mostar

septembar/september 1993

Foto: Studio HADŽIĆ Mostar   oktobar/oktober 1993

therefore also unable to 'read' the city. The original meaning has vanished as well: a public space where people, to whatever religion they belong, get together; not just a physical, but also a psychological connection between the two sides of the river.

With the loss of this connection, the soul of the city has disappeared. While the rest of the city remains divided, this exact copy of the Old Bridge and the old center, together with its media attention, acts like there were no division at all, and denies its recent history. The bridge seems to have been restored too early because its connecting function is not part of its current meaning. In contrast to many other buildings in Mostar that have not been rebuilt yet, the shape and image of the bridge have been restored, but not its meaning. That makes the poignant question, which Bogdan Bogdanović has posed after the demolition of the Old Bridge, even more important: "This leads us to the inevitable question whether we understand what the irreversible disappearance of a city brings about. If the city is an unsurpassed storage place for memories, one that by far surpasses the memories of a nation, race, and language, what will be the consequences of that disappearance?"

Foto: Studio HADŽIĆ Mostar

novembar/november 1993

Foto: Studio HADŽIĆ Mostar

mart/march 2005

Still, to this day, architecture is being used as a weapon to keep the city divided and impose political ideas. Mostar was once a clear repository of symbols and memories; now the city has become hazy, almost opaque. An abundance of fragmented and imaginary, self-proclaimed, and self-imposed commemorations are being added to the city's fabric.

Currently, it is impossible to walk through Mostar without being confronted with the war. At the same time the citizens have changed after the war; the past is being retold and emphasized in competing ways by symbolic architectural interventions. The communication between the city-dwellers and Mostar itself, has ceased to exist, as history is no longer clearly visible in the architecture and the public spaces. Due to destroyed buildings and added political and religious symbols, it is impossible for the inhabitants to wave the war away, to deal with it, and to forgive. Since a younger generation of citizens who did not experience the war directly is not able to meet each other and engage in a dialog, prejudices will live on. How can the psychological recovery from the war continue and how can people deal with their history when they are constantly confronted with destroyed buildings and with new religious and political symbols of division in public space? Will the citizens of Mostar ever be able to read their city again?

What else remains after the death of a city? The rubble, the survivors, and many memories. Memories not only located within Mostar, but dispersed among the many countries that the inhabitants fled to. In his book *From Summer to Reality*, Chris Keulemans refers to Dubravka Ugrešić, a Croatian author who explains the possible modes of survival during and after the Bosnia-Herzegovina War:
"Somebody who has to live through a war can choose from three modes of survival: adaption, inner exile, or fleeing. All three are a kind of tour of the underworld, which has to be made in order to reconquer the right to a new life. All three demand from a survivor the discarding of his old life, of the habits and preferences from which it was made, the characteristics by which his environment could recognize him."[19]
The decline and destruction of the conventional industries, the unemployment, decay, and empty spaces of the city center, coupled with an unsafe

environment, drove young and educated people away from the city. The absences provided by the people who fled, combined with the addition of refugees from the surrounding rural areas, created a new social structure for Mostar.

Bullet Holes as Ornaments

The effects of the destruction during the war can be divided into two categories: physical and psychological consequences. The physical ones are the most visible: roofs, building frames, windows, and parts of façades have been blown away by grenades and bullets, destroying buildings and creating vacant dwellings next to the streets that are full with grenade shell holes. Neglected for a long time, their interiors are overgrown and their walls are often covered in graffiti. As the ruins are slowly eroded by climatic influences, the scars from the wars become even more visible. This does not only result in a horrifying image, but also a fascinating one. Interiors become exteriors and part of the public space. Those who dare can enter the buildings and might even appreciate their new characteristics. As susceptible materials did not endure the war, the buildings reveal their robust constructions: the basic shapes of their architecture. The thousands of scars from grenade shells and bullet holes have become ornaments. Even so, these buildings should not be considered as romantic ruins. Their destruction is not the result of neglect or abandonment, but of a sudden, deliberate annihilation.

A destroyed building tells a story: it shows a transformation in time, but most importantly it leaves a lot to one's own imagination. Suddenly, a building is shrouded in mystery. This environment of destruction is not just fascinating, but also a daily remembrance of the war, which has direct psychological consequences. How can one commence one's own mental reconstruction when the physical environment is destroyed? The inhabitants will not be able to put these memories of war to rest as long as the destroyed buildings are a daily reminder of the war. Moreover, the divisions within the city, although these have been removed physically, continue to exist as mental boundaries, such as the Boulevard. The persistence of these mental boundaries is highlighted by a TV program entitled *Perspektiva*, made by Radio Slobodna Evropa together with The National Endowment for Democracy (NED), on the way young people in the Balkans deal with sensitive subjects. One of the episodes was on Mostar, in which teenagers from both sides of the city were interviewed. They talked about their fears of going to 'the other side' of the city. In this program, one Catholic boy explains that he has never gone to the other side because he is afraid. In the program, he is persuaded to cross the Old Bridge and drink a cup of coffee in the old city. Afterwards he confesses that he, "didn't feel uncomfortable, no one was unkind to me. It felt normal, I didn't have the idea that I was different from the other people and I am happy that I went and I hope we young people will not transfer the hatred onto our children." This shows that, although the war finished twenty years ago, it continues to have a profound impact, even on the children who never even

Mostar's Central Zone with on the left the Gymnasium and on the right the old Glass Bank Building.

experienced it. It greatly influences the way they move in the city and the way they relate to each other.

(Re)constructions: separate and equal

Apart from the physical changes that took place during the war, Mostar had to deal with transformations of other kinds as well. Gradually after the war, not only many of the buildings were restored, but also the local government of the city had to be reestablished. The division of Mostar was addressed by the Washington Agreement, which had put an end to the war between the Bosnian army and the Croatian Republic of Herzeg-Bosnia, and the European Union was issued a mandate to govern the city for a period of two years. The European Union Administration of Mostar (EUAM) was installed and aimed to maintain peace, facilitate the return of refugees, and restore essential institutions in the city.

Two years later, when the mandate of the EUAM ended, the Office of the High Representative (OHR) was founded in order to develop new strategies for unifying the city. As part of this, an interim statute of the city was established as a temporary solution for the city's self-governance. The statute allowed the city to be separated into a Croatian and a Muslim part. Seven large autonomous districts were created: three in the West with a Croatian majority, three in the East with a Muslim majority, and a small commonly governed Central Zone. Mostar city center contained three of these seven divided districts: the Croatian governed Southwest District, the Muslim governed Old City and in between the Croatian and Muslim districts, the Central Zone. The interim statute also appointed a central city government, with a mayor, a deputy mayor, and a city council.

Each district had its own urban planning authority and started simultaneously,

The thousands of scars from grenade shells and bullet holes
are visible in the many ruins still standing in Mostar.

but separately, without consulting each other, to rebuild parts of the city.
As it was the only politically shared space, the EUAM hoped that the Central
Zone could be an area where interaction and discussion between the two
ethnicities could take place. They hoped that soon the Interim Statute would
be replaced by a permanent statute and that the Central Zone could be the
physical starting point for a reunited city. This zone covered an important
part of the city, which resulted in fierce discussions about its borders. It was
disputed whether specific symbols or economically vital places should also
be a part of this area.

The two most important places that were not part of the Central Zone were
the Liska Street cemetery, which contained both Muslim and Croatian graves,
and the water supply. Both were assigned to the authority of the Croatian
districts. However, the Gymnasium and the bus and train station were part of
the Central Zone. Due to the resistance of the Croatian-controlled districts,
the size of this Central Zone turned out to be much smaller than was initially
hoped by the EUAM and the Muslim-controlled districts. This reduction in
size was seen as impairing the chances of future unification.

Between 1997 and 2003, several attempts were made to unite the public
services of education and medical infrastructure without any success. In
2003 a commission was founded that was dedicated to reforming the city
and handling the problematic division. The six districts as governing units were
abolished and replaced by a single city government. The interests of the
districts, however, were maintained by turning them into constituencies. In
2011, the constitutional court declared the current statute as unconstitutional

because the number of representatives of the constituencies did not correlate with the numbers of voters in each district. The city has been waiting for a new statute ever since.

The aforementioned developments resulted in a very complex political climate, hindering the process of rebuilding. Many postwar reconstruction projects have reflected these difficulties. The reconstruction of deliberately destroyed public and religious buildings raised questions and controversies. The debates on the different identities and the tendencies of separation and unification came to be implemented in the architecture and public spaces. Many religious symbols and monuments have been added to public space. Streets have received new, often 'nationalist' names, and ethnically and politically colored institutions have been given prominent places in the city. Social and cultural anthropologist Dr. Monika Palmberger describes it as follows: In terms of street names in Mostar, it is necessary to distinguish between East and West Mostar. While in the former, street names for the most part remained the same as they had been before 1992, street names in the latter underwent considerable renaming. Today, street names, newly erected memorials, and religious symbols mark the public space of West Mostar as part of the Croat nation. The claim that Mostar is an exclusively Croat city goes so far that the Bosnian east side of the city is simply ignored, e.g. in books or on maps of Mostar. Interestingly, a study of Mostar's tourist guides conducted by Pilvi Torsti revealed that Bosnian tourist guides continue to present the entire city similar to before the war, while Croat guides concentrate only on West Mostar and leave the Ottoman heritage, such as the Old Town, unmentioned. The new street names emphasize a shared history of the motherland of Croatia by recalling Croat historic personalities and important Croat cities. The communist past was erased by 'Croatianizing' them. For example, the street once called Omladinska (Street of the Youth) was renamed Hrvatske mladeži (Croat Youth). The simple message behind this was that Croats should no longer be reminded of the communist youth (which might bring up fond memories of being a member of the Yugoslav Pioneers) and should instead direct their feelings and affection exclusively towards the Croat youth. A similar example is Trg Rondo, a central roundabout and square in West Mostar, which was renamed Trg Hrvatskih Velikan – Trg Mate Bobana (Croat Nobles Square – Mate Boban Square). Although this square has been renamed, the majority of people still refer to it by its former and simpler name Rondo. Rondo is also the location of a cultural center formally called Dom kulture (House of Culture). Today, big letters on the top of the building proclaim its new name: Hrvatski dom herceg Stjepan Kosača (Croat House – Duke Stjepan Kosač).[20]

The Central Zone, however, the public space that should be most shared in Mostar, is subject to the biggest controversies regarding the (re)construction of buildings. One example is the Gymnasium, which was heavily bombed during the war. Built during the Austro-Hungarian era, the building is considered to have housed one of the best high schools of Yugoslavia before the war. Because it is located in the Central Zone it was intended to be a shared space for the inhabitants of both Croatian and Muslim districts. No discussion was dedicated to the way it would be rebuilt: it needed to look exactly like it did before the war. In 2000, the Croatian District only reconstructed the first floor of the building and reopened it as the Brother Dominik Mandić Grammar School. Naming the school after a Franciscan friar made it clear that the school was exclusively meant for Catholic Croats. The Office of the High Representative (OHR) responded by deciding that once the entire school building would be reconstructed, both Croatian and Muslim-run schools should be housed there. Under the catchphrase of 'separate but equal schools', the two institutions would share the same roof and function apart from each other: each with their own board, curriculum, students, and entrances.

In 2003, when the new Old Bridge was being restored and the political unification of Mostar came closer, the OHR and the Organization for Security and Co-operation in Europe (OSCE) proposed to merge the boards of the two schools, as well as the mathematics and science curricula. From that point onwards, the two schools in the Gymnasium shared the same name, board, and physical building. Yet the students were still being taught separately, except for the mathematics and science curricula.
In 2006, the United World College (UWC) of Mostar moved in to the third floor. This high school aims to contribute to the reconstruction of postwar societies by way of education. It has students from many different ethnic backgrounds from former Yugoslavia, as well as many countries in southern, eastern and western Europe, the Middle East, the USA, and many other crisis countries like Israel and Lebanon. It is astounding that a single structure can hold such a vast quantity of contradiction, divisions, and unities and still support its own weight.

Despite the single city government established in 2003, Mostar remains culturally and socially separated to a large extent to this day. The Central Zone, which for a decade was the physical border between the two ethnicities, has now become a buffer zone. A kind of no man's land that cannot be ignored because it is located at the heart of the city. After the political reunification of the city, it somehow remains a neglected area to be avoided by all. There is little there: neither shared spaces, nor many private ones. While regulations and decisions about whether construction projects for the area will continue to remain in limbo, so does the fate of Mostar's former Central Zone.[21]

Map of Mostar

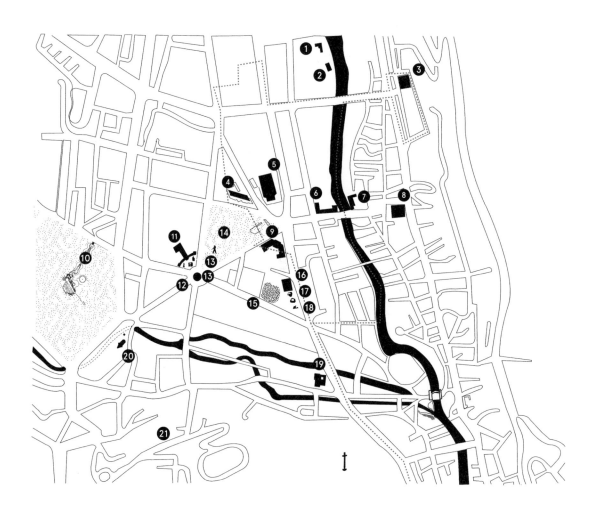

Locations on this map from above, left to right:

1. Waterworks building
2. Local swimming pool
3. Train and bus station
4. Glass Bank building
5. Former Hit department store
6. Hotel Bristol
7. Hotel Neretva
8. Razvitak department store
9. Gymnasium
10. Partisan Necropolis
11. House of Culture/House of Croats
12. Monuments to Marko Marulić and Queen Katarina Kosača Kotromanić

13. Monument to the fallen Croat defendors
14. Bruce Lee monument
15. Liska Street Cemetery
16. City Hall
17. Monuments for the Croat Defence Council
18. Monument for fighters of the Bosnian Army
19. Catholic Cathedral
20. Franciscan Church
21. Jubilee Cross on Hum Hill

Added symbols
in Mostar's public space

Monument to Hungarian S-FOR
soldiers that helped rebuilding
the Old Bridge, 2012

The Friendship Fountain, 2003

Monument for the Croat
Defence Council, 2012

Monument for fighters of the Bosnian
Army, 2012

Monument to Marko Marulić, 2005

Monument to Queen Katarina
Kosača Kotromanić, 2005

Bruce Lee statue as a symbol of
solidarity, 2005

Monument to the Fallen Croat
Defenders, 2004

Spanish Square, a monument
to eighteen killed Spanish
peacekeepers, 1998

Franciscan church, 1872 & 2004

Catholic Cathedral, 2004

Jubilee Cross, 2000

"*They say that history repeats itself, but history is only history, you haven't heard my story yet.*"

Sun Ra in *A Joyful Noise*

The city has existed for centuries, longer than generations, longer than languages, and many powers and religions have found refuge here. Throughout that time, memories and events of the city have been built layer upon layer. Most citizens are probably aware of the past of the city, but history is slippery: not all historical layers are visible and some are only subtly present. The reason why some urban public spaces function so well in some particular parts of the city is that the function of a particular building is embedded historically and spatially. The infrastructure, surrounding architecture, pavement, and greenery are set to complement each other. A psychological image of architectural buildings and their functions are branded in people's minds. While a city may change physically, the psychological image is not easily altered. For Mostar, however, the recent history of war has severely affected both the physicality and the psychological image of the city. By structuring a completely new image based on a subjective interpretation of history, the city is incomprehensible to its citizens. A city, by nature, is of course not based on one truth or one layer, but consists of a varied and rich past. This layered history should be visible in the architecture and public space of the city. It should not be imposed upon the citizens by bringing the city back to its exact original state, or by reconstructing or even copying buildings in their old style. Rather, the reconstruction of the city should be based on the many layers of the city's cultural history, particularly in a city where war has changed so much. These layers are important because they offer different historical points of reference to people from different backgrounds and with different views. It shows its nuances and origin as a gradual process. In this way, people can appropriate the buildings and fill them with meaning in their own way.

Nowadays, every building, every monument, and every street name in Mostar is ethnically and politically charged. In a society where the past and memory itself have become so vague, and have become subject to politics, we have to look for a new language, a clean language that nobody will politically, religiously, or ethnically identify themselves with. A language that does not ignore or deny the past, but engages with it and puts it into a new perspective without imposing one truth. A language that looks to the future, like the monuments commemorating the victims of World War II in former Yugoslavia.

This new language could be compared to the way the designer Jurgen Bey describes the beauty of the language of art that exists within the reader: "It is an open language that does not seal things, but a language that, if you listen to it, provides potential, and because of that can work as an accelerator. The beauty of the language of art is that it is much closer to literature. Everybody who reads a book knows that the language only exists with him or her. Everything you know comes forward; anything you do not know doesn't exist."[22]

The biggest design challenge for Mostar lies—apart from the obvious necessary architectural tasks like the (re)building or renovating of houses, hospitals, schools, parks, etc.—in forming a new open architectural language where the meaning and experience of space can exist within the reader. This language cannot just be applied to any piece of architecture or public space, or acquire every possible function for use. Regarding the rebuilding of destroyed buildings, it is necessary to make a distinction between buildings with political, religious, or ethnic significance before the war, and buildings without. It is important that architecture charged with these kinds of meanings manifests the different layers of its history. Ruins of buildings do not always have to be cleared. In the same manner, exact copies of pre-war buildings are undesirable. Also, building completely new architectural structures may be meaningless. Rather, parts of the ruined structure can become layers within the renovation process. By not filling in all the psychological and physical parts of the puzzle, an open language offers the opportunity for one's own imagination. The more fragmented memories of its history that are incorporated into the rebuilding of a structure, the more clues there are for relating to it.

The opportunities lie, for the most part, also in buildings that did not have any significant political, religious, or ethnic meaning before the war. Everything that was viewed as 'meaningless' was left untouched during the war. These sites and structures continue to exist as 'open' places that are neutral and unburdened by the past. Places that can mold the potential of a new future. The Central Zone—the part of the city that should be an entirely 'open' place—consists of a number of these places, such as the Glass Bank building. For the construction of completely new buildings on ahistorical sites, the opportunities lie in constructing something that is not burdened by religion, politics, or ethnicity, but that instead is closer to the creativity and individualism of the arts. As these buildings would employ a new architectural language, their function should be mostly public and aimed at facilitating encounters between people. This new architectural language need not remove any symbols. Bogdan Bogdanović used symbols for the monuments he designed throughout Yugoslavia that transcended ethnicity and religion in order to avoid making any political or ideological statements. Instead, he found his inspiration in ancient shapes and kept diving deeper into the richness of archetypical images. He tried to reach the primal shapes of the imagination. We can learn a lot from Bogdan Bogdanović's efforts when deciding on new functions of these neutral and inclusive places. What if we

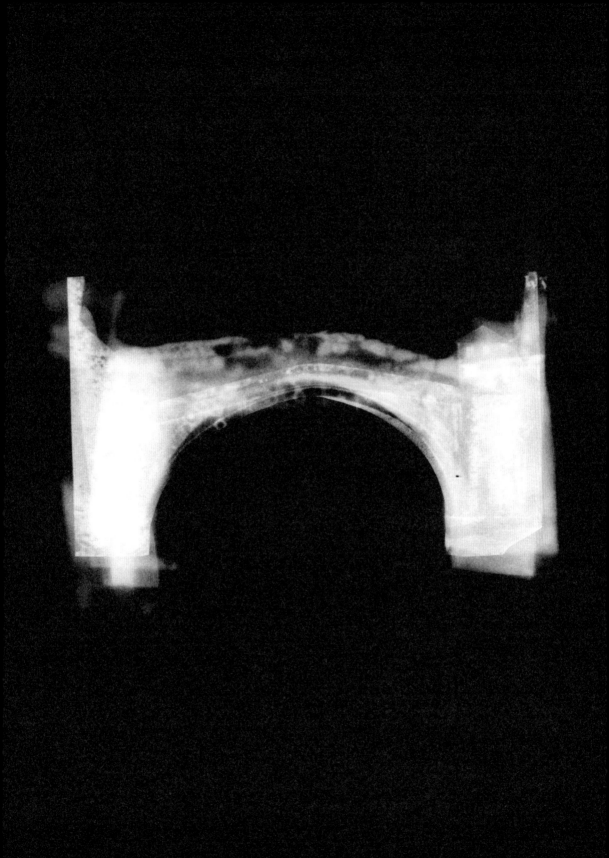

The Old Bridge from 1992–2013.

focused on functions that have to do with ancient traditions that go beyond any specific religion or ethnicity? To get there, it is important to thoroughly investigate and recognize the cultural, historical, and spatial qualities of Mostar—those that do not refer to ethnicity and religion. Currently this design language is largely absent in architecture and urban planning. In theater and music, however, there are a couple of examples that employ a new open language liberated from politics or ethnicity. The Mostarki Teater Mladih (the Mostar Youth Theater) educates young people in practical drama and production, and is open to anyone, regardless of their ethnicity or religion. Experimentation, openness, development, and bridging differences are a way of working and a life philosophy for the members of the theater group.

The Mostar band Zoster—which named itself after the *Herpes zoster* virus and rose to fame in the aftermath of the autoimmune disease that afflicted its society—tries to add tolerance, peace, development, and love to the music scene of Bosnia-Herzegovina. This band, which was founded in 2000, has experimented with many musical styles and has become increasingly abstract in their language and expressions over the years. Mario Knezović, the band's front man and singer, has stated that he does not want to impose a message on his audience. When listening to their music, I can find many references that point towards the political, social, and economic situation of Bosnia-Herzegovina and Mostar. However, the stance of Zoster is precisely to remain neutral in their lyrics. With their music they convey things without saying them. They keep things open in order for listeners to appropriate them. When I asked Knezović if the message of his lyrics would have been different had he grown up in another city, he hesitated, but eventually stuck to his point: it is not about the message, it is about opening up, offering neutrality and an opportunity for thought to hold on to. This seems the best possible strategy for Mostar: not to force people to be together, but to offer them opportunities for thought and new perspectives on history, as well as the present, and future. It would probably also be the best approach to apply to the urban planning of Mostar. An area similar to the former neutral zone cannot function when it appeals to only one specific group of people, but will only work when it is neutral, when it allows people to make it their own by employing an open language. That is why it is essential to implement an architectural intervention that is grounded on precisely this stance: not taking any stance.

Mostar currently finds itself in an exceptional condition. Like any other city, it will never again be the way it is right now or has been. What we can be sure of is that the city will never be like the pre-war image people have of it. It will instead change into a totally different city. The way a city like Mostar will rebuild itself is unclear. The inhabitants of the city have a great responsibility in this regard; they share something in the unique images of destruction and are able to contribute to the building of a new society. Instead of equally dividing public buildings and public space for both parts of the city, including

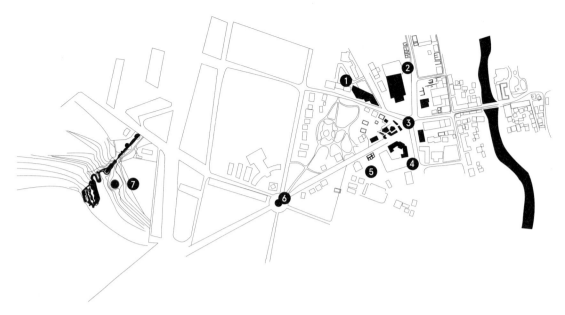

Current urban situation in Mostar:

1.   Glass Bank building
2.   Old Hit department store,
     now the fundation of
     the Croatian National Theater
3.   Spanish square

4.   Gymnasium
5.   Old library
6.   Rondo
7.   Partisan Necropolis

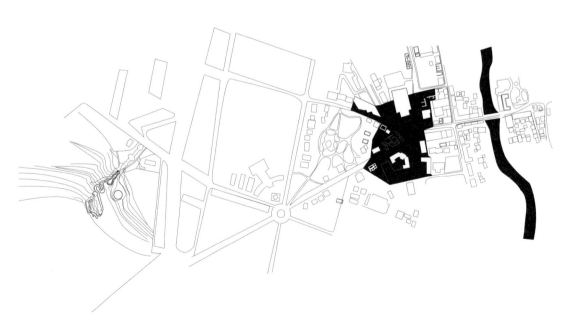

Proposed situation: plan of the elevated square as a catalyst for an open
language in the public space of Mostar.

schools, fire departments, cellular networks, hospitals, football teams, and bus stations, they should try to build towards a shared and inclusive society where there is space for everyone's own interpretation, regardless of one's religion or background. In this way, public buildings and public space can promote more than only one history, one truth, one religion, or one group of people.

As intended by the EU, the Central Zone is an area appropriated to reconstruct public and shared buildings. I propose doing this in a way that employs an open language. As of yet, the process of rebuilding in this area is slow, difficult, and full of struggles: Today, Croatian, Muslim, and international students are all being taught separately in the Gymnasium that has been entirely brought back to its original state. The Glass Bank building is still in ruins, and because it never had any religious or ethnic meaning, it is considered to 'not have enough significance' to be reconstructed. The old library is also still in ruins. Before the war, it had an important public meaning and it is currently unclear what its future function should be once it has been reconstructed. At the spot where the Hit department store used to be, there is now the unfinished first floor of what was to become the Croatian National Theater. However, construction was halted in 2002 because its program had focused on one particular group of people or religion and therefore threatened the neutrality of the zone. The junction between the Gymnasium, the Hit department store and the Glass Bank building—informally referred to as Hit— was named 'Spanish Square' in 1998, following the construction of a monument dedicated to the eighteen Spanish peacekeepers who were killed in and around Mostar during the war. Renaming this square to commemorate Spanish peacekeepers is an example of European interference in this area. While the financial and structural help from different EU countries has been beneficial to Mostar, once again it seems that meaning is imposed upon its citizens without truly taking its context into consideration. These examples show that the opportunity to build an inclusive city together has not been taken. While each of these buildings are potentially able to appeal to the different groups of people living in Mostar, instead they have now followed a different renovation strategy, resulting in a fragmentation of meaning.

As a design intervention, I propose that the public space of the Central Zone, should be a large open square. This would be a slightly elevated, paved area in order to show the contours of this shared space, where demolished buildings, renovated buildings, and buildings that are (re)constructed are all present. All of these buildings have a prospective public function. On the elevated square, buildings either face the square or are located on it as solitary elements. The square is clearly delimited, but it is still possible to move onto other important public spaces in the city, such as the Zrinjevac Parc, Rondo, Tito's bridge, Musala square, and the Old City. Because the streets are incorporated in the elevated square, it causes people to have to use them as public spaces as well, instead of just merely as ways of getting somewhere. This square would not be a proper microcosm of Mostar without a bar or restaurant, which I propose to locate at the heart of the square, where the buildings intersect.

With these urban interventions as foundations, on the following pages, I will provide the outline for a number of interventions to take place on the square, with an open language that has the backbone of an old tradition belonging to Mostar.

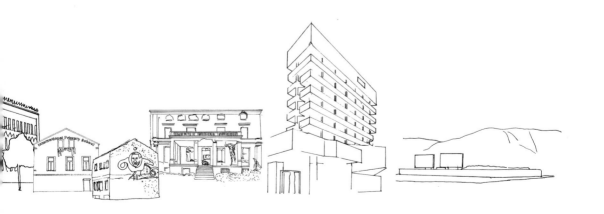

By gradually altering the square within the Central Zone layer by layer, citizens will slowly adjust to the changing public spaces of the city. Inserting a variety of references that allow them to read the history of the buildings that surround them will increase the probability for them to read their city again. By identifying with them, and by appropriating them, the citizens of Mostar might slowly find common ground again. The next step, however, is to reach a higher level, namely writing the city. In order for the citizens to actually be able to write the city again, we need to go back to the traits and codes of conduct that belong to living in a city and urban life. By recalling their own traditions, which never completely disappeared but may have been put on hold for one generation, the citizens of Mostar should listen to their own memories. These memories could be based on old urban traditions that were and still are the premises for the city to function, as 'promenading' along the Korzo and public street cabaret (Liskaluk) once were, and like jumping off the Old Bridge still is. This is the only way to write the city again.

Immortal moments
Diving off of the Old Bridge used to be a ritual where young men dove off the bridge to prove their manliness and impress young women. Boys learned step by step how to dive and ultimately become skilled enough to jump off the Old Bridge. A diving contest is still held every year, where the most famous international high board divers take the plunge. This urban activity has remained a shared tradition and is practiced by people from all religious backgrounds. This public activity may be a perfect way to connect people once again.

In order to form a new operational architectural language in the 'neutral' zone, I propose a building that includes a diving school where citizens can learn, step by step, to dive from great heights with the plunge from the new Old Bridge as the final step. By designing such a place, an urban activity is made available to all the inhabitants of the city, regardless of their nationality, religion, gender, age, or sexual orientation. It is not just diving off the Old Bridge, but also diving itself that is an age-old tradition. Diving is something atavistic. It is pre-religious. Historians question whether jumpers found on pre-Christian paintings could actually swim. It may be that diving even predates swimming.

Diving from the springboard in the old city pool of Mostar.

Shaping the public spaces to accommodate new urban and inclusive activities is essential. Especially in the present circumstances shaped by the destruction of the last war, room must be made for public activities. By creating a number of anchor points in public spaces, the area could develop itself further from there. On the elevated square, with the Gymnasium, the diving place, and a café as anchor points, a new Korzo could arise, with the history of Mostar in all its diversity as its background. The diving school will be located at the square, right at the spot where the old Hit department store used to be, which is currently occupied by the unfinished Croatian National Theater. The building will face the Gymnasium. This school, which teaches (although separate from each other) both Croatian, Muslim, and international students, is directly opposite the building. Because all groups and nationalities already use this building, and since this entire area already possesses a public history, it is a very appropriate location to construct a building where people can learn to dive from great heights. The building itself is more of a sculpture or monument than a building. Just like the monuments that commemorate the victims of the Second World War, it is relatively accessible and has no windows, doors, or roofs. It is an open public space and has four sides that are all directed towards a particular area of the square. The entrance is located on the north side of the square and consists of paving that resembles a carpet that leads up the huge stairs, with two wings that point in both directions. The steps are 50 centimeters high, which means that people can advance step by step—each time 50 centimeters higher—to a greater jumping height. These steps can also function as a grandstand to sit on or gather before the jumping, with the north side of Mostar as its backdrop. With every 50 centimeters they ascend, the steps also get 50 centimeters wider on both sides, so that they extend like wings. These two sides are meant for practice, up to 17.5 meters high. One side faces the Glass Bank Building and the entrance of the park, the other the Old Bank Building and the road towards Tito's bridge. The end of the stairs reaches 18 meters in height and is the endpoint for practice before moving to jumping off the Old Bridge. This last step spans the entire length and faces towards the Gymnasium and the Spanish Square. At street level, the spectators are separated from the water by a wall of 50 centimeters height. In this way, both adults and children can witness the diver entering the water. At the same time the wall can function as a public seating area.

In Mostar, diving off the Old Bridge is a tradition that has its origin in the very structure of the city. Without the existence of the Old Bridge, the tradition would never have been there. Even after the war when the Old Bridge was demolished and before there was a stand-in bridge, there was a springboard from which people could dive into the river. The jump is a form of survival for the inhabitants of Mostar, it is something they can hold on to, because it forms the foundation of being a Mostarac or Mostarka, not just a member of some district. The sensation of weightlessness is the feeling of 'eternity', something without limits, infinite, oceanic. Furthermore, swimming is an

important and meaningful part of diving. Swimming has to be taught or else one is bound to drown. Everything one undertakes to overcome this condition could be explained as the continuous battle against one's natural instincts: to sink.[23]

Swimming teaches us to keep our heads above water. Jumping off the bridge is an individual activity, but one that makes connections between men, as equals, through the courage to do so. The three-second jump towards the water provides a feeling of weightlessness and freedom where one becomes detached from everything around oneself, including one's entanglement in the struggles of Mostar; an empowerment to conquer the city and the architecture for a moment and dive into the future with a new version of the old one in mind.

Design intervention: a building with diving as its function
and as an open public space, seen from the front.

The 50-centimeter-high steps enable people to advance step by step—
each time 50 centimeters higher—to a greater jumping height.

Conclusion

From Mostar to Amsterdam, Beirut and Stockholm

An interview with Arna Mačkić by Rosa te Velde

RV   Rosa te Velde
AM   Arna Mačkić

RV   You have told me it took you years before you had the strength and knowledge to take Mostar as your research topic. *Mortal Cities & Forgotten Monuments* presents a highly personal history. At times you speak in a detached way about the ruins and the war, while in other passages your tone of voice seems to be more emotional. How did your research change your relationship with Mostar?

AM   In August 2014, when I was almost finished with my project, I visited Mostar once again. The year before, I had completely immersed myself in the way architecture and public space are used and abused to construct a particular identity. Only parts of history, specific memories, and symbols are used to selectively create this identity. The city's reconstruction after the war is still ongoing, and therefore the war is ever present. I used to be angry, frustrated, and sad when visiting Mostar. Just like Bogdanović, I realized that Mostar was a mortal city and that it had 'died' due to the war and its consequences. Before, I just couldn't accept these changes. But now I understand the politics much better. I still find it difficult to be faced with the traces of the war, but what is most striking is the continuation of the war through architecture that divides rather than unites. While the 'abuse' of architecture as a way of maintaining a divide within the city is strongly present, my thorough research has offered me a deeper understanding, and with it, also some kind of peace of mind. Being aware of the politics of architecture, the use of symbols, and the strategy of making many of the memories invisible, made me realize that the present situation only demonstrates one truth of the many to which I can choose to relate. The others might just not be visible, but with the knowledge I have gained, I am free to bring them to the surface. Although many trips will follow, this journey felt like an appropriate conclusion to my research. I was gradually able to understand my own history from a new perspective, allowing me to see friends, family, and places in a different context.

RV   How did you continue your research?

AM   After presenting my research through different platforms like *Failed Architecture* and *Eurozine*, I noted that a larger audience shared interest in this topic. To my surprise, I was invited by the Swedish Färgfabriken (a museum of art, architecture, and urban development) to do a series of lectures in Beirut. While I did realize before that architectural post-war problems would not be exclusive to Mostar, it was only there that I grasped the urgency and global scope of the topic of building inclusive and uniting architecture as one of the restoring tools after wartime. Moreover, I recognized that many Western European cities are dealing more and more with the issue of identity: heritage and identity are extremely sensitive topics nowadays, due to the economic and migration crises facing Europe. Cities become segregated on a variety of levels: 'place branding', gentrification, neoliberalism, and right-wing ideology seem to cleanse cities of their diversity. I therefore argue that designing diverse and open identities through architecture is crucial. It is possible to grasp and transform their exclusive character by firstly investigating the way local and governmental politics control how public spaces express particular identities, and secondly investigating the multiplicity of the histories of these places.

RV   What are the similarities and differences between Beirut and Mostar that you noticed during your first visit to Beirut?

AM   Similar to Mostar, the atmosphere in Beirut is charged. Although it was my first time in Beirut, I was lucky to be introduced to the city by locals and was therefore able to see through the hospitality of the inhabitants, but also the cruel remnants that are everywhere and the current division in the city. After Lebanon's independence from France in 1943, the parliament was officially divided in equal measure between Muslims and Christians; however, the tensions between many more religious minorities grew over the years. The Lebanese Civil War that lasted from 1975 to 1990 and the 2005 War between Hezbollah and Israel left deep marks on the architectural surroundings. Cultural heritage was strategically destroyed during wartime, but is rebuilt precisely as if no war had ever happened, just like in Mostar. Some of the sites of cultural heritage have been selectively rebuilt, depending on their significance to the ruling power. However, most of these places are mainly used by

tourists today, who are inevitably unaware of the tragic history of these places. Other destroyed sites are mostly used to rebuild architecture that is extremely nationalist or religious. What is also strongly present is a tendency to exploit the lots for extremely costly and commercial buildings. The urban planning and redevelopment of Beirut is monopolized by Solidere, an extremely powerful company founded in 1994 by the then Prime Minister Rafik Hariri that enjoys special political advantages. One of their projects is the Beirut Souqs. Although referring to the old Arabic open-air markets, this area is an exclusive and expensive shopping district. The central district of Beirut has become extremely privatized. Even many of the parks and beaches are not accessible. Taking away the much needed breathing spaces and room to maneuver in this crowded city seems to be a strategy to paralyze the citizens and prevent them from being free, civilized human beings.

RV   How is your research relevant to a city like Amsterdam?

AM   It seems that various parts of the center of Amsterdam are increasingly becoming more or less the same. The power of private developers is quickly reshaping Amsterdam's city center. Many architects seem to be slavishly executing plans made by developers. The gimmicky use of references to history is ubiquitous in their designs (see for example the Foodhallen), but these are often bland attempts to 'inject' their designs with identity.
This exclusive and homogeneous architecture pushes the less fortunate to the outskirts, much in the same way as in other gentrified cities like Beirut or New York. The city center is gradually growing into a happy open-air museum where tourists stroll and only the very rich reside. The canals seem to be frozen in time and

are arguably a copy from the seventeenth century—to which we gladly refer as the glorified 'Golden Age' rather than the age of the colonies and slavery. This is highly problematic, as people of Surinamese, Antillean, and Indonesian descent have little to relate to when considering Amsterdam's architectural design. Thanks to former Dutch Prime Minister Jan-Peter Balkenende, referring to the 'VOC mentality' has become a common way, mostly in politics, to emphasize the alleged entrepreneurial spirit of the Dutch. Ironically, many of the ships sailing for the Dutch East India Company (VOC, Vereenigde Oostindische Compagnie) were manned by crews that comprised men from throughout Europe and of whom only as little as 15 percent were Dutch. This is indicative of the selective and tainted picture that is created in the media and public discourse.

Many architects are not interested in delving into the many different and sometimes ambiguous histories of an area, or truly investigating how everyone could read it. Of course I understand that they 'have to do their jobs', meaning: they have to take on the assignments of these developers. But what I don't see is a little more interest in or awareness of the way these building projects may offer opportunities to create architecture and public spaces that are truly public. I would argue that all cities in Western Europe have their own dark pages in history, whether dating from the First or Second World War, the Cold War or perhaps their colonial past, yet these are topics that are skillfully ignored by architects. They are simply not present in the current design vocabulary of most designers and architects. In other words, my research of Mostar is also highly relevant to a place like Amsterdam because the tendency to 'copy' history in a selective and exclusive way is dominant here as well. Amsterdam is not as divided or segregated as Mostar, but it soon may be.

RV What are your thoughts on maintaining a little more diversity in Amsterdam and creating a public space that allows different people to 'read' and 'write' the city?

AM To test my ideas, I worked within the team of RAAAF [Rietveld Architecture-Art-Affordances] to develop a proposal for Amsterdam's formal navy yard. In the seventeenth century, this area served as the gateway to the world. It was from here that ships would depart to our colonies and discover new worlds. Cultures, knowledge, and products were exchanged. The Netherlands in general has more than a few dark pages in its history, which are ignored as much as possible. The current tendency to formulate 'our' identity, as rightwing politicians do in the face of the poignant migration crisis, is very exclusive and employs history for legitimization. However, the history of this navy yard can potentially highlight the versatility of our global histories. In order to redefine 'diversity', we have proposed an educational intervention for this terrain, addressing schoolchildren in particular. Amsterdam presumably has the most mixed and diverse schools in the Netherlands. Many schools are trying to deal with the way they can foster mutual understanding among their pupils. However, the design of the city ignores youngsters: there are very few public spaces that are built to actually appeal to them. Rather than addressing a particular ethnicity as the target audience for this project, I feel that the category of 'schoolchildren' redefines the established categories of social reality. We suggest building a campfire and a large compass, thereby encouraging the children to reflect on their own and each other's pasts. Before visiting the navy yard with their class, each of the children is given the task of finding out about the lives of their grandmother's grandmother. Where did she come from and what did her life look like?

The compass is used to turn the needle in the right direction to imagine their location. While freeing them from being 'Moroccan' or 'Surinamese', this project deals with the 'other' side of history in a positive way and may contribute to an awareness of (the history of) diversity in the Netherlands. If you don't know the way the Netherlands has been connected and dependent on its global connectedness, and if these relationships are systematically ignored or not expressed by our built environment, it encourages simplistic feelings of nationalism.

RV I know you have a personal preference for the abstract and sometimes futuristic architecture of for example Bogdanović—and rightly so in my view. Many architects have their own vision of what good design means to them visually and conceptually. But what role does formal language play in the case of designing for inclusivity? How does one avoid imposing some kind of imperialist view of what good design should be and how can one make it appeal to everyone?

AM That is indeed a difficult issue. I will of course never be able to design in some kind of language that is free from a particular expression: my own preferences will always be at play. Recalling the designs by Bogdanović, we can see how he avoided particular delicate symbols, and although exceptional, his designs are—naturally— the products of a zeitgeist. Therefore it is impossible to even think that a design language exists that appeals to everyone. However, I hope that by focusing on the history of and relevance to a particular audience, the design language is 'open' enough to appeal to them. Moreover, another strategy is to avoid symbols that evoke negative connotations, and instead search for other more 'open' and positive symbols.

RV How are you planning to continue from here? What would be your ultimate goal?

AM I would love to continue my research by inviting designers, historians, sociologists, artists, scholars, and anyone interested in developing alternatives to the current approach to heritage in both Western cities and in cities that have been destroyed by war. There has only been limited study of the consequences of architecture on the way identities are shaped and vice versa. The bottom line is to find alternatives for the empty, simplistic, and selective approach to dealing with identity and history, as conducted by many architects and urban developers. If we don't even try to find alternatives, we build mortal cities. It may be challenging, but if no alternative examples are set, it is hard for others to follow. Involving many different perspectives and including various voices and disciplines also has a beneficial effect on the content, as, needless to say, it adds layers of knowledge and complexity to a project. By sharing my interests and taking a curious stance, I hope to inspire others to be reflective on the topic of diversity and inclusive design. I believe that educating young architects, organizing symposiums, and writing articles nurtures my practice as an architect and creates important momentum in raising public awareness and support. Also, I aspire to expand my own design practice as much as possible. I don't believe an architect can do any good by working alone in his studio: it is ultimately an extremely social profession.

Epilogue
Nura & Zlatko Mačkić

It was a time in which we never could have guessed the kind of tribulations that would lie ahead of us.

The first years of Arna's life were carefree; years of playing with her brother, sister, and many other children. Though quiet by nature, Arna also proved to be very communicative by showing her creativity through all sorts of games.

Unfortunately these times did not last long. A typhoon of war began to engulf our country. Everything changed, child's play not excepted. Fear started to nestle itself in the heads of little children, who suddenly grew up overnight. They realized that something terrible was happening, but they did not understand why. A period started, of sirens signifying the threat of bombardments, of running to bomb shelters, of father's time in the concentration camp, and eventually of expulsion.

The first encounter with the Netherlands was the asylum center full of refugees from different parts of the world. We were still confused and in shock, but glad to be in safe territory and to be able to provide our children with the opportunity to go to school again. A time of adapting to new living conditions and of learning a new language began. We soon moved to Zoetermeer, to a flat with over 300 apartments, and once again we had to adapt to a new school and a new multicultural environment.

From day one, Arna was a diligent pupil at her new school and always got good marks. After finishing her high school education she applied for the Gerrit Rietveld Academie and moved to Amsterdam.

This short description shows how different Arna's youth was from that of most other children who have had the luck of not having to witness a war, who have been able to grow up with peace and security.

Arna Mačkić, Jasenovac, 2013.

All of this has definitely left its traces on Arna. It has made her stronger, and at the same time influenced her future, her choice of profession. For a long time our Arna tried to find a way of finding the best possible way to express her feelings through creativity and to present them to others. We are convinced that she has found this by choosing architecture as a profession. The reason for this was that Arna always wanted to

do something that is not just interesting, but
also meaningful, and useful. We are very glad
to know that she does this with a lot of love
and enjoyment.

During our first visit to her country of birth, Arna
realized that the way of living and communicating
as it existed before the war has ceased to exist.
People have separated themselves into groups,
based on their religion and ethnicity. Mostar
is an extreme example of this. A lot has been
destroyed. A city that used to be a place for
everybody and that served as the paragon of
living together has disappeared. Old symbols,
old landmark buildings, old public places have
disappeared and were replaced by new symbols
and buildings. The appearance of the city has
changed, and with it the past and the soul
of Mostar.

Precisely this has had its influence on Arna's
decision to—as far as her capabilities extend—
do something that can once again unite people;
for them to live next to each other, and not be
separated by the Neretva River, and once again
can meet in shared schools, theaters, and cafés...

Through this project, Arna tells the story of her
youth, which ended far too soon—the story of
the people and the country where she was born,
and the story of the hope for a better future for
the city and its inhabitants.

Footnotes

1   Bogdanović B. (1994), *Grad I smrt, Beogradski krug Beograd*, p. 8.

2   Gunzburger Makaš E. (2007), *Representing competing identities: Building and rebuilding in postwar Mostar, Bosnia-Herzegovina*, p. 347.

3   Markovina, R. (2013), "Moj Mostar kakvoga volim i pamtim", Tacno.net, http://tacno.net/mostar/roko-markovina-moj-mostar-kakvoga-volim-i-pamtim/ [trans.]

4   Gunzburger Makaš E. (2007), *Representing competing identities: Building and rebuilding in postwar Mostar, Bosnia-Herzegovina*, p. 13.

5   Gunzburger Makaš E. (2007), *Representing competing identities: Building and rebuilding in postwar Mostar, Bosnia-Herzegovina*, p. 138.

6   Gunzburger Makaš E. (2007), *Representing competing identities: Building and rebuilding in postwar Mostar, Bosnia-Herzegovina*, p. 188.

7   Robert Bevan, *The Destruction of Memory, Architecture at War*, London: Reaktion Books, 2006, p.8 & p. 46.

8   Kundera M., *The book of laughter and forgetting*, Czechoslovakia, 1979

9   K. Šego, I. Ribarević-Nikolić, Ž. Jurić, V. Kolopić et al., *Mostar '92 Urbicid*, Mostar, Hrvatsko vijeće općine, 1992, p. 27. (translated by Arna Mackic and Janno Martens)

10   Robert Bevan, *The Destruction of Memory, Architecture at War*, London: Reaktion Books, 2006, p. 8 & p. 46.

11   Keulemans C., *Van de zomer naar de werkelijkheid*, Amsterdam: Uitgeverij de Balie, 1997, pp. 60-65.

12   Miličević-Nikolić O., *Spomen-groblje u Mostaru. □ovjek i prostor*, n. 168, 1967, pp. 6-18.

13   Charles Merewether, "Traces of Loss", in: Michael Roth, Claire Lyons, Charles Merewether (eds.) *Irresistible Decay*, Los Angeles: Getty Institute, 1997, pp. 25-40.

14   Herbert Muschamp, "The Commemorative Beauty of Tragic Wreckage", *The New York Times*, Sunday issue, November 11, 2001, p. 37.

15   Christopher Woodward, *In Ruins*, London (Vintage) 2001, p. 23/24.

16   John Ruskin, *Seven Lamps of Architecture*, Boston (Dana Estes Company) 1890, "Lamp of Memory", p. 185.

17   Ian Travnor, "Bridge opens but Mostar remains a divided city", *The Guardian*, 2004. http://www.theguardian.com/world/2004/jul/23/iantraynor

18   http://whc.unesco.org/en/list/946

19   Keulemans C., *Van de zomer naar de werkelijkheid*, Amsterdam: Uitgeverij de Balie, 1997, p. 100.

20   Palmberger M., *Renaming of Public Space: A Policy of Exclusion in Bosnia and Herzegovina*, 2012, pp. 14-18.

21   Gunzburger Makaš E., *Mostar's Central Zone: Battles over Shared Space in a Divided City*, 2011, pp. 1-10.

22   Jurgen Bey, quote from the debate series "In de Toekomstige Tijd: Utopisch denken in het onderwijs".

23   Van Leeuwen T.A.P., *The Springboard in the Pond*, 2000, p. 14.

Image credits

Imprint

Concept and writing
Arna Mačkić

Graphic design
Bas Koopmans
Nuno Beijinho
Oliver Modosch

Copy editing
Rosa te Velde
Ben Liebelt

Proofreading
Selene States

Translation
Janno Martens
Arna Mačkić

Lithography, printing, and binding
DZA Druckerei zu Altenburg GmbH, Altenburg

Acknowledgments
In loving memory of Kimeta Muminagić

Chris Bakker, Lorien Beijaert, Bastiaan Bervoets,
Anne Ardina Brouwers, Meintje Delisse, Failed Architecture,
Vibeke Gieskes, Uri Gilad, Carsten Goertz, Jan Haeck,
Rob Hootsmans, Onno Kamer, Mario Knezović, Nura Mačkić,
Zlatko Mačkić, Qaisar Mahmood, Janno Martens, Mark Minkjan,
Saša Radenović, Ronald Rietveld, Erik Rietveld, Luuc Sonke,
Daniel Urey, Maarten Vermeulen, Barbara Visser, Elke van
Waalwijk van Doorn

Arna Mačkić is an architect based in Amsterdam.
www.mortalcitiesforgottenmonuments.com

Park Books AG
Niederdorfstrasse 54
8001 Zurich
Switzerland
www.park-books.com

ISBN 978-3-03860-009-1